SpringerBriefs in Computer Science

T0259906

For further volumes:
http://www.springer.com/series/10028

Kan Yang · Xiaohua Jia

Security for Cloud Storage Systems

 Springer

Kan Yang
Xiaohua Jia
Department of Computer Science
City University of Hong Kong
Kowloon
Hong Kong SAR

ISSN 2191-5768   ISSN 2191-5776   (electronic)
ISBN 978-1-4614-7872-0   ISBN 978-1-4614-7873-7   (eBook)
DOI 10.1007/978-1-4614-7873-7
Springer New York Heidelberg Dordrecht London

Library of Congress Control Number: 2013939832

Printed on acid-free paper

Springer is part of Springer Science+Business Media (www.springer.com)

Preface

Cloud storage is an important service of cloud computing, which offers services for data owners to host their data in the cloud. This new paradigm of data hosting and data access services introduces two major security concerns: (1) Protection of data integrity. Data owners may not fully trust the cloud server and worry that data stored in the cloud could be corrupted or even removed. (2) Data access control. Data owners may worry that some dishonest servers give data access to unauthorized users, such that they can no longer rely on the servers to conduct data access control. In this book, we investigate the security issues in the cloud storage systems and develop secure solutions to ensure data owners the safety and security of the data stored in the cloud.

We first introduce Third-party Storage Auditing Service (TSAS), an efficient and secure dynamic auditing service to ensure the cloud data integrity in Chap. 2. In Chap. 3, we describe Attribute-Based Access Control (ABAS), a fine-grained access control scheme with efficient attribute revocation for cloud storage systems. In Chap. 4, we further present Data Access Control for Multi-Authority Cloud Storage (DAC-MACS), a data access control scheme with efficient revocation and decryption for cloud storage systems with multiple authorities.

We hope this book gives the reader an overview of the data security for cloud storage systems, and will serve as a good introductory reference to improve the security of cloud storage systems.

Hong Kong, March 2013
Kan Yang
Xiaohua Jia

Acknowledgments

The authors would like to thank Dr. Kui Ren at University at Buffalo, The State University of New York, for his valuable suggestions and comments on our works. We also would like to thank Dr. Zhen Liu at City University of Hong Kong for his help in Attribute-based Encryption.

We are also grateful for the assistance provided by Courtney Clark and the publication team at SpringerBriefs.

Contents

Chapter 1
Introduction

Abstract Cloud computing has emerged as a promising technique that greatly changes the modern IT industry. In this chapter, we first give a brief introduction to cloud storage systems. Then, we explore some security issues in cloud storage systems, including data integrity and data confidentiality. We also give an overview on how to solve these security problems.

1.1 Brief Introduction to Cloud Storage Systems

1.1.1 Cloud Computing

Cloud computing has emerged as a promising technique that greatly changes the modern IT industry. The National Institute of Standards and Technology (NIST) defined the cloud computing as follows [12].

> *Cloud computing is a model for enabling convenient, on-demand network access to a shared pool of configurable and reliable computing resources (e.g., networks, servers, storage, applications, services) that can be rapidly provisioned and released with minimal consumer management effort or service provider interaction.*

This cloud model is composed of **five** *essential characteristics*, **three** *service models*, and **four** *deployment models*.

The five essential characteristics are defined as

- On-demand self-service
- Ubiquitous network access
- Resource pooling

K. Yang and X. Jia, *Security for Cloud Storage Systems*, SpringerBriefs
in Computer Science, DOI: 10.1007/978-1-4614-7873-7_1,
© The Author(s) 2014

- Rapid elasticity or expansion
- Measured service

  The service models are defined as

- Cloud Software as a Service (SaaS)—Use providers applications over a network.
- Cloud Platform as a Service (PaaS)—Deploy customer-created applications to a cloud.
- Cloud Infrastructure as a Service (IaaS)—Rent processing, storage, network capacity, and other fundamental computing resources.

The deployment models, which can be either internally or externally implemented, are summarized in the NIST definition as

- Private cloud—Enterprise owned or leased
- Community cloud—Shared infrastructure for specific community
- Public cloud—Sold to the public, mega-scale infrastructure
- Hybrid cloud—Composition of two or more clouds

1.1.2 Cloud Storage as a Service

Cloud storage is an important service of cloud computing, which allows data owners (owners) to host data from their local computing systems to the cloud. Cloud storage is a model of networked online storage where data is stored in virtualized pools of storage which are generally hosted by third parties (e.g., the storage service providers). The service providers operate large data centers, and data owners buy or lease storage capacity from them in a pay-as-you-go business model. The service providers, in the background, virtualize the resources according to the requirements of the customer and expose them as storage pools, which the customers can themselves use to store files or data objects. Physically, the resource may span across multiple servers.

The cloud storage can provide a comparably low-cost, scalable, location independent platform for managing users data, thus more and more data owners start to store the data in the cloud [1]. By hosting their data in the cloud, data owners can avoid the initial investment of expensive infrastructure setup, large equipments, and daily maintenance cost. The data owners only need to pay the space they actually use, e.g., cost-per-gigabyte-stored model [17]. Another reason is that data owners can rely on the cloud to provide more reliable services, so that they can access data from anywhere and at any time. Individuals or small-sized companies usually do not have the resource to keep their servers as reliable as the cloud does.

However, this new paradigm of data storage service also introduces new security challenges. The principal goal of this book is to investigate the security issues in the cloud storage systems and develop secure solutions to ensure data owners the safety and security of the data stored in the cloud.

1.2 Data Security for Cloud Storage Systems

When people outsource data into the cloud, they cannot manage the data as in their local storage systems. On the other hand, because service providers are not in the same trust domain as data owners, they cannot be fully trusted by data owners. Therefore, the cloud storage system introduces two major security concerns: (1) Protection of data integrity. Data owners may worry that data stored in the cloud could be corrupted or even deleted. (2) Data access control. Data owners may worry that some dishonest servers give data access to unauthorized users.

1.2.1 Storage Auditing as a Service

When outsourcing data in the cloud, data owners would worry their data could be lost or corrupted in the cloud. This is because data loss could happen in any infrastructure, no matter what high degree of reliable measures the cloud service providers would take [2, 15]. Some recent data loss incidents are the Sidekick Cloud Disaster in 2009 [4] and the breakdown of Amazon's Elastic Compute Cloud (EC2) in 2010 [13]. Sometimes, the cloud service providers may be dishonest and they may discard the data which has not been accessed or rarely accessed to save the storage space or keep fewer replicas than promised. Moreover, the cloud service providers may choose to hide data loss and claim that the data are still correctly stored in the cloud. As a result, data owners need to be convinced that their data are correctly stored in the cloud.

Checking on retrieval is a common method for checking the data integrity, which means data owners check the data integrity when accessing their data. This method has been used in peer-to-peer storage systems [7, 14], network file systems [6, 8], long-term archives [11], web-service object stores [20] and database systems [10]. However, *checking on retrieval* is not sufficient to check the integrity for all the data stored in the cloud. There is usually a large amount of data stored in the cloud, but only a small percentage is frequently accessed. There is no guarantee for the data that are rarely accessed. An improved method was proposed by generating some virtual retrievals to check the integrity of rarely accessed data. But this causes heavy I/O overhead on the cloud servers and high communication cost due to the data retrieval operations.

Therefore, it is desirable to have storage auditing service to assure data owners that their data are correctly stored in the cloud. But data owners are not willing to perform such auditing service due to the heavy overhead and cost. In fact, it is not fair to let any side of the cloud service providers or the data owners conduct the auditing, because neither of them could be guaranteed to provide unbiased and honest auditing result [18]. Third party auditing is a natural choice for the storage auditing. A third party auditor who has expertise and capabilities can do a more efficient work and convince both the cloud service provider and the data owner. On one hand, through the auditing reports released by the third party auditor, data owners can make sure that their data is correctly stored in the cloud. On the other hand, the cloud service provider can also build a good reputation from good auditing reports and enhance its competitiveness. This book aims to design an efficient third party auditing scheme for cloud storage systems.

1.2.2 Access Control as a Service

In cloud storage systems, data owners would worry their data could be mis-used or accessed by unauthorized users. However, the data access control is a challenging issue in cloud storage systems, because the cloud storage service separates the roles of the data owner from the data service provider, and the data owner does not interact with the user directly for providing data access service.

Existing methods [16] usually delegate data access control to a trusted server and let it be in charge of defining and enforcing access policies. However, the cloud server cannot be fully trusted by data owners, since the cloud server may give data access to unauthorized users to make more profit (e.g., the competitor of a company). Thus, traditional server-based data access control methods are no longer suitable for cloud storage systems.

To achieve data access control on untrusted servers, traditional methods usually require the data owner to encrypt the data m with a symmetric content key K by using symmetric encryption method, and encrypt the content key K with each user's public key PK_u by using public encryption methods. Since the data owner delegates the data access service to the remote server, the data owner does not need to stay online "24/7/365" to distribute the content key to all the users. Thus, the ciphertext of the content key $E_{PK_u}(K)$ (the encrypted forms of the content key) will be stored on the server together with the encrypted data $E_K(m)$. The user can retrieve both the ciphertext of the content key $E_{PK_u}(K)$ and the encrypted data $E_K(m)$. However, in cloud storage systems, it is very difficult for data owners to know all the potential users beforehand [5, 9], and thus data owners cannot encrypt the content key with all the users' public keys or predefine a fixed access control list for the data. Moreover, the storage overhead on the server caused by the ciphertext of the content key is linear with the total number of all the users in the system.

The Ciphertext-Policy Attribute-based Encryption (CP-ABE) [3, 19] is regarded as one of the most suitable technologies for data access control in cloud storage systems, because it gives the data owner more direct control on access policies and the policy checking occurs "inside the cryptography". In CP-ABE scheme, there is an authority that is responsible for attribute management. Each owner in the system is associated with a set of attributes that describe its role or identity in the system. To encrypt a file, the data owner first defines an access policy over the universal attribute set, and then encrypts it under this access policy. Only the users whose attributes satisfy the access policy are able to decrypt the ciphertext. However, due to the *attribute revocation problem*, it is very costly to apply the CP-ABE approach to control the data access in cloud storage systems.

This book aims to study the data access control issue in cloud storage systems, where the data owner is in charge of defining and enforcing the access policy.

References

1. Armbrust, M., Fox, A., Griffith, R., Joseph, A.D., Katz, R.H., Konwinski, A., Lee, G., Patterson, D.A., Rabkin, A., Stoica, I., Zaharia, M.: A view of cloud computing. Commun. ACM **53**(4), 50–58 (2010)
2. Bairavasundaram, L.N., Goodson, G.R., Pasupathy, S., Schindler, J.: An analysis of latent sector errors in disk drives. In: Proceedings of the 2007 ACM SIGMETRICS International Conference on Measurement and Modeling of Computer Systems (SIGMETRICS'07), pp. 289–300. ACM, New York (2007)
3. Bethencourt, J., Sahai, A., Waters, B.: Ciphertext-policy attribute-based encryption. In: Proceedings of the 2007 IEEE Symposium on Security and Privacy (S&P'07), pp. 321–334. IEEE Computer Society, Los Alamitos (2007)
4. Cellan-Jones, R.: The Sidekick Cloud Disaster. BBC News, vol. 1 (2009)
5. Gouglidis, A., Mavridis, I.: On the definition of access control requirements for grid and cloud computing systems. In: Proceedings of the 3rd International ICST Conference on Networks for Grid Applications (GridNets'09), pp. 19–26. Springer, New York (2009)
6. Kallahalla, M., Riedel, E., Swaminathan, R., Wang, Q., Fu, K.: Plutus: scalable secure file sharing on untrusted storage. In: Proceedings of the 2nd USENIX Conference on File and Storage Technologies (FAST'03). USENIX, Berkeley (2003)
7. Kubiatowicz, J., Bindel, D., Chen, Y., Czerwinski, S.E., Eaton, P.R., Geels, D., Gummadi, R., Rhea, S.C., Weatherspoon, H., Weimer, W., Wells, C., Zhao, B.Y.: Oceanstore: an architecture for global-scale persistent storage. In: Proceedings of the 9th International Conference on Architectural Support for Programming Languages and Operating Systems (ASPLOS'00), pp. 190–201. ACM Press, New York (2000)
8. Li, J., Krohn, M.N., Mazières, D., Shasha, D.: Secure untrusted data repository (sundr). In: Proceedings of the 6th conference on Symposium on Operating Systems Design and Implementation, pp. 121–136. USENIX, Berkeley (2004)
9. Lomet, D.B.: Guest editor's introduction: cloud data management. IEEE Trans. Knowl. Data Eng. **23**(9), 1281 (2011)
10. Maheshwari, U., Vingralek, R., Shapiro, W.: How to build a trusted database system on untrusted storage. In: Proceedings of the 4th conference on Symposium on Operating System Design and Implementation, pp. 135–150. USENIX, Berkeley (2000)
11. Maniatis, P., Roussopoulos, M., Giuli, T.J., Rosenthal, D.S.H., Baker, M.: The LOCKSS peer-to-peer digital preservation system. ACM Trans. Comput. Syst. **23**(1), 2–50 (2005)
12. Mell, P., Grance, T.: The NIST definition of cloud computing. Technical report, National Institute of Standards and Technology (2009)
13. Miller, R.: Amazon Addresses EC2 Power Outages. Data Center Knowledge, vol. 1 (2010)
14. Muthitacharoen, A., Morris, R., Gil, T.M., Chen, B.: Ivy: a read/write peer-to-peer file system. In: Proceedings of OSDI (2002)
15. Schroeder, B., Gibson, G.A.: Disk failures in the real world: What does an mttf of 1,000,000 hours mean to you. In: Proceedings of the 5th USENIX Conference on File and Storage Technologies (FAST'07), pp. 1–16. USENIX, Berkeley (2007)
16. Sohr, K., Drouineaud, M., Ahn, G.J., Gogolla, M.: Analyzing and managing role-based access control policies. IEEE Trans. Knowl. Data Eng. **20**(7), 924–939 (2008)
17. Velte, T., Velte, A., Elsenpeter, R.: Cloud Computing: A Practical Approach, 1st edn. McGraw-Hill Inc., New York (2010)
18. Wang, C., Ren, K., Lou, W., Li, J.: Toward publicly auditable secure cloud data storage services. IEEE Netw. **24**(4), 19–24 (2010)

19. Waters, B.: Ciphertext-policy attribute-based encryption: an expressive, efficient, and provably secure realization. In: Proceedings of the 4th International Conference on Practice and Theory in Public Key Cryptography (PKC'11), pp. 53–70. Springer, New York (2011)
20. Yumerefendi, A.R., Chase, J.S.: Strong accountability for network storage. In: Proceedings of the 5th USENIX Conference on File and Storage Technologies (FAST'07), pp. 77–92. USENIX, Berkeley (2007)

Chapter 2
TSAS: Third-Party Storage Auditing Service

Abstract In cloud storage systems, data owners host their data on cloud servers and users (data consumers) can access the data from cloud servers. Due to the data outsourcing, however, this new paradigm of data hosting service also introduces new security challenges, which requires an independent auditing service to check the data integrity in the cloud. In large-scale cloud storage systems, the data may be updated dynamically, so existing remote integrity checking methods served for static archive data are no longer applicable to check the data integrity. Thus, an efficient and secure dynamic auditing protocol is desired to convince data owners that the data is correctly stored in the cloud. In this chapter, we first introduce an auditing framework for cloud storage systems. Then, we describe Third-party Storage Auditing Scheme (TSAS), an efficient and privacy-preserving auditing protocol for cloud storage, which can also support data dynamic operations and batch auditing for both multiple owners and multiple clouds.

2.1 Introduction

Cloud storage is an important service of cloud computing [16], which allows data owners (owners) to move data from their local computing systems to the cloud. More and more owners start to store the data in the cloud [1]. However, this new paradigm of data hosting service also introduces new security challenges [24]. Owners would worry that the data could be lost in the cloud. This is because data loss could happen in any infrastructure, no matter what high degree of reliable measures cloud service providers would take [5, 11, 13, 14, 18]. Sometimes, cloud service providers might be dishonest. They could discard the data which has not been accessed or rarely accessed to save the storage space and claim that the data are still correctly stored in the cloud. Therefore, owners need to be convinced that the data are correctly stored in the cloud.

K. Yang and X. Jia, *Security for Cloud Storage Systems*, SpringerBriefs
in Computer Science, DOI: 10.1007/978-1-4614-7873-7_2,
© The Author(s) 2014

Traditionally, owners can check the data integrity based on two-party storage auditing protocols [6, 9, 12, 15, 17, 19, 20, 22, 28]. In cloud storage system, however, it is inappropriate to let either side of cloud service providers or owners conduct such auditing, because none of them could be guaranteed to provide unbiased auditing result. In this situation, *third party auditing* is a natural choice for the storage auditing in cloud computing. A third party auditor (auditor) that has expertise and capabilities can do a more efficient work and convince both cloud service providers and owners.

For the third party auditing in cloud storage systems, there are several important requirements which have been proposed in some previous works [25, 29]. The auditing protocol should have the following properties:

1. *Confidentiality* The auditing protocol should keep owner's data confidential against the auditor.
2. *Dynamic Auditing* The auditing protocol should support the dynamic updates of the data in the cloud.
3. *Batch Auditing* The auditing protocol should also be able to support the batch auditing for multiple owners and multiple clouds.

Recently, several remote integrity checking protocols were proposed to allow the auditor to check the data integrity on the remote server [2, 4, 8, 21, 26, 27, 30–32]. Table 2.1 gives the comparisons among some existing remote integrity checking schemes in terms of the performance, the privacy protection, the support of dynamic operations and the batch auditing for multiple owners and multiple clouds. Table 2.1 shows that many of the existing schemes are not privacy-preserving or cannot support the data dynamic operations, so that they cannot be applied to cloud storage systems.

In [27], the authors proposed a dynamic auditing protocol that can support the dynamic operations of the data on the cloud servers, but this method may leak the data content to the auditor because it requires the server to send the linear combinations of data blocks to the auditor. In [26], the authors extended their dynamic auditing scheme to be privacy-preserving and support the batch auditing for multiple owners.

Table 2.1 Comparison of remote integrity checking schemes

Scheme	Computation		Commu-	Privacy	Dynamic	Batch operation		Prob. of
	Sever	Verifier	nication			Multi-owner	Multi-cloud	detection
PDP [2]	$O(t)$	$O(t)$	$O(1)$	Yes	No	No	No	$1 - (1 - \rho)^t$
CPDP [21]	$O(t + s)$	$O(t + s)$	$O(t + s)$	No	No	No	No	$1 - (1 - \rho)^{ts}$
DPDP [8]	$O(t \log n)$	$O(t \log n)$	$O(t \log n)$	No	No	No	No	$1 - (1 - \rho)^t$
Audit [27, 26]	$O(t \log n)$	$O(t \log n)$	$O(t \log n)$	Yes	Yes	Yes	No	$1 - (1 - \rho)^t$
IPDP [31, 32]	$O(ts)$	$O(t + s)$	$O(t + s)$	Yes	Yes	No	Yes	$1 - (1 - \rho)^{ts}$
TSAS	$O(ts)$	$O(t)$	$O(t)$	Yes	Yes	Yes	Yes	$1 - (1 - \rho)^{ts}$

n is the total number of data blocks of a file; t is the number of challenged data blocks in an auditing query

s is the number of sectors in each data block; ρ is the probability of block/sector corruption (suppose the probability of corruption is the same for the equal size of data block or sector)

However, due to the large number of data tags, their auditing protocols may incur a heavy storage overhead on the server. In [31], Zhu et al. proposed a cooperative provable data possession scheme that can support the batch auditing for multiple clouds and also extended it to support the dynamic auditing in [32]. However, their scheme cannot support the batch auditing for multiple owners. That is because parameters for generating the data tags used by each owner are different and thus they cannot combine the data tags from multiple owners to conduct the batch auditing. Another drawback is that their scheme requires an additional trusted organizer to send a commitment to the auditor during the multi-cloud batch auditing, because their scheme applies the mask technique to ensure the data privacy. However, such additional organizer is not practical in cloud storage systems. Furthermore, both Wang's schemes and Zhu's schemes incur heavy computation cost of the auditor, which makes the auditor a performance bottleneck.

In this chapter, we introduce Third-party Storage Auditing Service (TSAS) to ensure the data integrity in the cloud, where all the above listed requirements are satisfied. To solve the data privacy problem, the method in TSAS is to generate an encrypted proof with the challenge stamp by using the *Bilinearity* property of the bilinear pairing, such that the auditor cannot decrypt it but can verify the correctness of the proof. Without using the mask technique, it does not require any trusted organizer during the batch auditing for multiple clouds. On the other hand, the auditing protocol lets the server compute the proof as an intermediate value of the verification, such that the auditor can directly use this intermediate value to verify the correctness of the proof. Therefore, it can greatly reduce the computing loads of the auditor by moving it to the cloud server.

2.2 Preliminaries and Definitions

2.2.1 Bilinear Pairing

Let $\mathbb{G}_1$, $\mathbb{G}_2$ and $\mathbb{G}_T$ be three multiplicative groups with the same prime order p. A bilinear map is a map $e : \mathbb{G}_1 \times \mathbb{G}_2 \rightarrow \mathbb{G}_T$ with the following properties:

1. Bilinearity: $e(u^a, v^b) = e(u, v)^{ab}$ for all $u \in \mathbb{G}_1$, $v \in \mathbb{G}_2$ and $a, b \in \mathbb{Z}_p$.
2. Non-degeneracy: There exist $u \in \mathbb{G}_1$, $v \in \mathbb{G}_2$ such that $e(u, v) \neq I$, where I is the identity element of $\mathbb{G}_T$.
3. Computability: e can be computed in an efficient way.

Such a bilinear map is called a bilinear pairing.

2.2.2 Computational Bilinear Diffie-Hellman Assumption

The definition of the Computational Bilinear Diffie-Hellman (CBDH) assumption is defined as follows.

A challenger chooses a group $\mathbb{G}$ of prime order p according to the security parameter. Let $a, b, c \in \mathbb{Z}_p$ be chosen at random and g be a generator of $\mathbb{G}$. When given g, g^a, g^b, g^c, the adversary must compute $e(g, g)^{abc}$.

An algorithm $\mathcal{B}$ that outputs $e(g, g)^{abc}$ has advantage ε in solving CBDH in $\mathbb{G}$ if

$$|Pr[\mathcal{B}(g, g^a, g^b, g^c) = e(g, g)^{abc}]| \geq \varepsilon.$$

Definition 2.1 The (t, ε)-CBDH assumption holds if no t-time algorithm has a nonnegligible probability ε in solving the CBDH problem.

2.2.3 Definition of System Model

As shown in Fig. 2.1, an auditing system for cloud storage normally involves data owners (owner), the cloud server (server) and the third party auditor (auditor). The owners create the data and host their data in the cloud. The cloud server stores the owners' data and provides the data access to users (data consumers). The auditor is a trusted third party that has expertise and capabilities to provide data storage auditing service for both the owners and servers. The auditor can be a trusted organization managed by the government, which can provide unbiased auditing result for both data owners and cloud servers.

Before describing the auditing protocol definition, some notations are defined as in Table 2.2.

Definition 2.2 (TSAS). TSAS is a collection of the following five algorithms: KeyGen, TagGen, Chall, Prove and Verify.

- **KeyGen**$(\lambda) \rightarrow (sk_h, sk_t, pk_t)$. This key generation algorithm takes no input other than the implicit security parameter λ. It outputs a secret hash key sk_h and a pair of secret-public tag key (sk_t, pk_t).
- **TagGen**$(M, sk_t, sk_h) \rightarrow T$. The tag generation algorithm takes as inputs an encrypted file M, the secret tag key sk_t and the secret hash key sk_h. For each

Fig. 2.1 System model of the data storage auditing

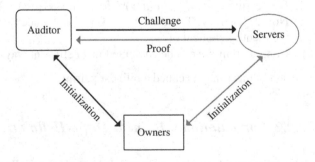

Table 2.2 Notations

Symbol	Physical meaning
sk_t	Secret tag key
pk_t	Public tag key
sk_h	Secret hash key
M	Data component
T	Set of data tags
n	Number of blocks in each component
s	Number of sectors in each data block
M_{info}	Abstract information of M
$\mathcal{C}$	Challenge generated by the auditor
$\mathcal{P}$	Proof generated by the server

data block m_i, it computes a data tag t_i based on sk_h and sk_t. It outputs a set of data tags $T = \{t_i\}_{i \in [1,n]}$.

- **Chall**$(M_{info}) \rightarrow \mathcal{C}$. The challenge algorithm takes as input the abstract information of the data M_{info} (e.g., file identity, total number of blocks, version number and timestamp etc.). It outputs a challenge $\mathcal{C}$.
- **Prove**$(M, T, \mathcal{C}) \rightarrow \mathcal{P}$. The prove algorithm takes as inputs the file M, the tags T and the challenge from the auditor $\mathcal{C}$. It outputs a proof $\mathcal{P}$.
- **Verify**$(\mathcal{C}, \mathcal{P}, sk_h, pk_t, M_{info}) \rightarrow 0/1$. The verification algorithm takes as inputs the $\mathcal{P}$ from the server, the secret hash key sk_h, the public tag key pk_t and the abstract information of the data M_{info}. It outputs the auditing result as 0 or 1.

2.2.4 Definition of Security Model

The auditor is assumed to be honest-but-curious. It performs honestly during the whole auditing procedure but it is curious about the received data. But the sever could be dishonest and may launch the following attacks:

1. *Replace Attack.* The server may choose another valid and uncorrupted pair of data block and data tag (m_k, t_k) to replace the challenged pair of data block and data tag (m_i, t_i), when it already discarded m_i or t_i.
2. *Forge Attack.* The server may forge the data tag of data block and deceive the auditor, if the owner's secret tag keys are reused for the different versions of data.
3. *Replay Attack.* The server may generate the proof from the previous proof or other information, without retrieving the actual owner's data.

2.3 An Efficient and Privacy-Preserving Auditing Protocol

In this section, we first present some techniques applied in the design of the auditing protocol. Then, we describe the algorithms and the detailed construction of the auditing protocol for cloud storage systems.

2.3.1 Overview

The main challenge in the design of data storage auditing protocol is the *data privacy problem* (i.e. the auditing protocol should protect the data privacy against the auditor.). This is because: (1) For public data, the auditor may obtain the data information by recovering the data blocks from the data proof. (2) For encrypted data, the auditor may obtain content keys somehow through any special channels and could be able to decrypt the data. To solve the data privacy problem, TSAS generates an encrypted proof with the challenge stamp by using the Bilinearity property of the bilinear pairing, such that the auditor cannot decrypt it. But the auditor can verify the correctness of the proof without decrypting it.

Although the auditor has sufficient expertise and capabilities to conduct the auditing service, the computing ability of an auditor is not as strong as cloud servers. Since the auditor needs to audit for many cloud servers and a large number of data owners, the auditor could be the performance bottleneck. TSAS lets the server compute the proof as an intermediate value of the verification (calculated by the challenge stamp and the linear combinations of data blocks), such that the auditor can use this intermediate value to verify the proof. Therefore, the computing loads of the auditor can be greatly reduced by moving it to the cloud server.

In TSAS, both the *Data Fragment Technique* and *Homomorphic Verifiable Tags* are applied to improve the performance. The data fragment technique can reduce number of data tags, such that it can reduce the storage overhead and improve the system performance. By using the homomorphic verifiable tags, no matter how many data blocks are challenged, the server only responses the sum of data blocks and the product of tags to the auditor, whose size is constant and equal to only one data block. Thus, it reduces the communication cost.

2.3.2 Algorithms for Auditing Protocol

Suppose a file F has m data components as $F = (F_1, \ldots, F_m)$. Each data component has its physical meanings and can be updated dynamically by the data owners. For public data components, the data owner does not need to encrypted it, but for private data component, the data owner needs to encrypt it with its corresponding key.

Each data component F_k is divided into n_k data blocks denoted as

$$F_k = (m_{k1}, m_{k2}, \ldots, m_{kn_k}).$$

Due to the security reason, the data block size should be restricted by the security parameter. For example, suppose the security level is set to be 160-bit (20-Byte), the data block size should be 20-Byte. A 50-KByte data component will be divided into 2,500 data blocks and generate 2,500 data tags, which incurs 50-KByte storage overhead.

By using the data fragment technique, each data block is further split into sectors. The sector size is restricted by the security parameter. One data tag is generated for each data block which consists of s sectors, such that it can reduce the number of data tags. In the same example above, a 50-KByte data component only incurs $50/s$ KByte storage overhead. In real storage systems, the data block size can be various. That is different data blocks could have different number of sectors. For example, if a data block m_i will be frequently read, then s_i could be large, but for those frequently updated data blocks, s_i could be relatively small.

For simplicity, the construction only considers one data component and constant number of sectors for each data block. Suppose there is a data component M, which is divided into n data blocks and each data block is further split into s sectors. For data blocks that have different number of sectors, it first selects the maximum number of sectors s_{max} among all the sector numbers s_i. Then, for each data block m_i with s_i sectors, $s_i < s_{max}$, it can simply consider that the data block m_i has s_{max} sectors by setting $m_{ij} = 0$ for $s_i < j \leq s_{max}$. Because the size of each sector is constant and equal to the security parameter p, the number of data blocks can be calculated as $n = \frac{sizeof(M)}{s \cdot \log p}$. The encrypted data component is denoted as $M = \{m_{ij}\}_{i \in [1,n], j \in [1,s]}$.

Let $\mathbb{G}_1$, $\mathbb{G}_2$ and $\mathbb{G}_T$ be the multiplicative groups with the same prime order p and $e : \mathbb{G}_1 \times \mathbb{G}_2 \to \mathbb{G}_T$ be the bilinear map. Let g_1 and g_2 be the generators of $\mathbb{G}_1$ and $\mathbb{G}_2$ respectively. Let $h : \{0, 1\}^* \to \mathbb{G}_1$ be a keyed secure hash function that maps the M_{info} to a point in $\mathbb{G}_1$.

The storage auditing protocol consists of the following algorithms:

- **KeyGen**$(\lambda) \to (pk_t, sk_t, sk_h)$. The key generation algorithm takes no input other than the implicit security parameter λ. It chooses two random number sk_t, $sk_h \in \mathbb{Z}_p$ as the secret tag key and the secret hash key. It outputs the public tag key as $pk_t = g_2^{sk_t} \in \mathbb{G}_2$, the secret tag key sk_t and the secret hash key sk_h.

- **TagGen**$(M, sk_t, sk_h) \to T$. The tag generation algorithm takes each data component M, the secret tag key sk_t and the secret hash key sk_h as inputs. It first chooses s random values $x_1, x_2, \ldots, x_s \in \mathbb{Z}_p$ and computes $u_j = g_1^{x_j} \in \mathbb{G}_1$ for all $j \in [1, s]$. For each data block $m_i (i \in [1, n])$, it computes a data tag t_i as

$$t_i = (h(sk_h, W_i) \cdot \prod_{j=1}^{s} u_j^{m_{ij}})^{sk_t},$$

where $W_i = FID\|i$ (the "$\|$" denotes the concatenation operation), in which FID is the identifier of the data and i represents the block number of m_i. It outputs the set of data tags $T = \{t_i\}_{i \in [1,n]}$.

- **Chall**$(M_{info}) \to \mathcal{C}$. The challenge algorithm takes the abstract information of the data M_{info} as the input. It selects some data blocks to construct the *Challenge Set* Q and generates a random number $v_i \in \mathbb{Z}_p^*$ for each chosen data block $m_i (i \in Q)$. Then, it computes the challenge stamp $R = (pk_t)^r$ by randomly choosing a number $r \in \mathbb{Z}_p^*$. It outputs the challenge as $\mathcal{C} = (\{i, v_i\}_{i \in Q}, R)$.

- **Prove**$(M, T, \mathcal{C}) \to \mathcal{P}$. The prove algorithm takes as inputs the data M and the received challenge $\mathcal{C} = (\{i, v_i\}_{i \in Q}, R)$. The proof consists of the *tag proof TP* and the *data proof DP*. The *tag proof* is generated as

$$TP = \prod_{i \in Q} t_i^{v_i}.$$

To generate the *data proof*, it first computes the sector linear combination of all the challenged data blocks MP_j for each $j \in [1, s]$ as

$$MP_j = \sum_{i \in Q} v_i \cdot m_{ij}.$$

Then, it generates the *data proof DP* as

$$DP = \prod_{j=1}^{s} e(u_j, R)^{MP_j}.$$

It outputs the proof $\mathcal{P} = (TP, DP)$.

- **Verify**$(\mathcal{C}, \mathcal{P}, sk_h, pk_t, M_{info}) \to 0/1$. The verification algorithm takes as inputs the challenge $\mathcal{C}$, the proof $\mathcal{P}$, the secret hash key sk_h, the public tag key pk_t and the abstract information of the data component. It first computes the identifier hash values $h(sk_h, W_i)$ of all the challenged data blocks and computes the challenge hash H_{chal} as

$$H_{chal} = \prod_{i \in Q} h(sk_h, W_i)^{rv_i}.$$

It then verifies the *proof* from the server by the following verification equation:

$$DP \cdot e(H_{chal}, pk_t) = e(TP, g_2^r). \tag{2.1}$$

If the above verification Eq. 2.1 holds, it outputs 1. Otherwise, it outputs 0.

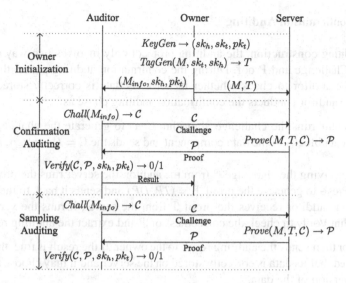

Fig. 2.2 Framework of the privacy-preserving auditing protocol

2.3.3 Construction of the Privacy-Preserving Auditing Protocol

As illustrated in Fig. 2.2, the storage auditing protocol consists of three phases: *Owner Initialization*, *Confirmation Auditing* and *Sampling Auditing*. During the system initialization, the owner generates the keys and the tags for the data. After storing the data on the server, the owner asks the auditor to conduct the confirmation auditing to make sure that their data is correctly stored on the server. Once confirmed, the owner can choose to delete the local copy of the data. Then, the auditor conducts the sampling auditing periodically to check the data integrity.

2.3.3.1 Owner Initialization

The owner runs the key generation algorithm KeyGen to generate the secret hash key sk_h, the pair of secret-public tag key (sk_t, pk_t). Then, it runs the tag generation algorithm TagGen to compute the data tags. After all the data tags are generated, the owner sends each data component $M = \{m_i\}_{i \in [1,n]}$ and its corresponding data tags $T = \{t_i\}_{i \in [1,n]}$ to the server together with the set of parameters $\{u_j\}_{j \in [1,s]}$. The owner then sends the public tag key pk_t, the secret hash key sk_h and the abstract information of the data M_{info} to the auditor, which includes the data identifier *FID*, the total number of data blocks n.

2.3.3.2 Confirmation Auditing

In the auditing construction, the auditing protocol only involves two-way communication: Challenge and Proof. During the confirmation auditing phase, the owner requires the auditor to check whether the owner's data is correctly stored on the server. The auditor conducts the confirmation auditing phase as

1. The auditor runs the challenge algorithm Chall to generate the challenge $\mathcal{C}$ for all the data blocks in the data component and sends the $\mathcal{C} = (\{i, v_i\}_{i \in Q}, R)$ to the server.
2. Upon receiving the challenge $\mathcal{C}$ from the auditor, the server runs the prove algorithm Prove to generate the proof $\mathcal{P} = (TP, DP)$ and sends it back to the auditor.
3. When the auditor receives the proof $\mathcal{P}$ from the server, it runs the verification algorithm Verify to check the correctness of $\mathcal{P}$ and extract the auditing result.

The auditor then sends the auditing result to the owner. If the result is true, the owner is convinced that its data is correctly stored on the server and it may choose to delete the local version of the data.

2.3.3.3 Sampling Auditing

The auditor will carry out the sampling auditing periodically by challenging a sample set of data blocks. The frequency of taking auditing operation depends on the service agreement between the data owner and the auditor (and also depends on how much trust the data owner has over the server). Similar to the confirmation auditing in Phase 2, the sampling auditing procedure also contains two-way communication as illustrated in Fig. 2.2.

Suppose each sector will be corrupted with a probability of ρ on the server. For a sampling auditing involved with t challenged data blocks, the probability of detection can be calculated as

$$Pr(t, s) = 1 - (1 - \rho)^{t \cdot s}.$$

That is this t-block sampling auditing can detect any data corruption with a probability of $Pr(t, s)$.

2.3.4 Correctness Proof

The correctness of the privacy-preserving auditing protocol is concluded as the following theorem:

Theorem 2.1 *In the proposed auditing protocol, the server passes the audit iff all the chosen data blocks and the data tags are correctly stored.*

Proof First, let's prove that if all the chosen data and the corresponding data tags are stored correctly on the server, the server will pass the auditing via the challenge-response protocol. The verification equation can be rewritten in details as the following:

$$
DP \cdot e(H_{chal}, pk_t) \tag{2.2}
$$

$$
= \prod_{j=1}^{s} e(u_j, R)^{MP_j} \cdot e(\prod_{i \in Q} h(sk_h, W_i)^{rv_i}, pk_t)
$$

$$
= \prod_{j=1}^{s} e(u_j, pk_t)^{r \prod_{i \in Q} v_i m_{ij}} \cdot e(\prod_{i \in Q} h(sk_h, W_i)^{rv_i}, pk_t)
$$

$$
= \prod_{i \in Q} e(\prod_{j=1}^{s} u_j^{m_{ij}}, pk_t^{rv_i}) e(h(sk_h, W_i), pk_t^{rv_i})
$$

$$
= \prod_{i \in Q} e(\prod_{j=1}^{s} h(sk_h, W_i) u_j^{m_{ij}}, pk_t^{rv_i})
$$

$$
= \prod_{i \in Q} e(\prod_{j=1}^{s} (h(sk_h, W_i) u_j^{m_{ij}})^{sk_t}, g_2^{rv_i})
$$

$$
= \prod_{i \in Q} e(t_i, g_2^{rv_i})
$$

$$
= e(TP, g_2^r)
$$

From Eq. 2.2, we can say that the server can pass the auditing, if the data blocks and the data tags are stored correctly on the server. However, if any of the challenged data block or data tag is corrupted or modified, the verification equation will not hold and the server cannot pass the audit.

2.4 Secure Dynamic Auditing

In cloud storage systems, the data owners will dynamically update their data. As an auditing service, the auditing protocol should be designed to support the dynamic data, as well as the static archive data. However, the dynamic operations may make the auditing protocols insecure. Specifically, the server may conduct two following attacks: (1) *Replay Attack* The server may not update correctly the owner's data on the server and may use the previous version of the data to pass the auditing. (2) *Forge Attack* When the data owner updates the data to the current version, the server may get enough information from the dynamic operations to forge the data tag. If the server could forge the data tag, it can use any data and its forged data tag to pass the auditing.

2.4.1 Solution of Dynamic Auditing

To prevent the replay attack, an *Index Table* (ITable) is introduced to record the abstract information of the data. The ITable consists of four components: *Index*, B_i, V_i and T_i. The *Index* denotes the current block number of data block m_i in the data component M. B_i denotes the original block number of data block m_i and V_i denotes the current version number of data block m_i. T_i is the timestamp used for generating the data tag.

This ITable is created by the owner during the owner initialization and managed by the auditor. When the owner completes the data dynamic operations, it sends an update message to the auditor for updating the ITable which is stored on the auditor. After the confirmation auditing, the auditor sends the result to the owner for the confirmation that the owner's data on the server and the abstraction information on the auditor are both up-to-date. This completes the data dynamic operation.

To deal with the forge attack, it can modify the tag generation algorithm TagGen. Specifically, when generating the data tag t_i for the data block m_i, the owners insert all the abstract information into the data tag by setting $W_i = FID||i||B_i||V_i||T_i$, such that the server cannot get enough information to forge the data tag from dynamic operations.

2.4.2 Algorithms and Constructions for Dynamic Auditing

The dynamic auditing protocol consists of four phases: Owner Initialization, Confirmation Auditing, Sampling Auditing and Dynamic Auditing.

The first three phases are similar to the privacy-preserving auditing protocol as described in the above section. The only differences are the tag generation algorithm TagGen and the ITable generation during the owner initialization phase. Here, Fig. 2.3 only illustrates the dynamic auditing phase, which contains three steps: Data Update, Index Update and Update Confirmation.

2.4.2.1 Data Update

There are three types of data update operations that can be used by the owner: Modification, Insertion and Deletion. For each update operation, there is a corresponding algorithm in the dynamic auditing to process the operation and facilitate the future auditing, defined as follows.

- **Modify**$(m_i^*, sk_t, sk_h) \rightarrow (Msg_{modify}, t_i^*)$. The modification algorithm takes as inputs the new version of data block m_i^*, the secret tag key sk_t and the secret hash key sk_h. It generates a new version number V_i^*, new timestamp T_i^* and calls the TagGen to generate a new data tag t_i^* for data block m_i^*. It outputs the new tag t_i^* and the update message $Msg_{modify} = (i, B_i, V_i^*, T_i^*)$. Then, it sends the new

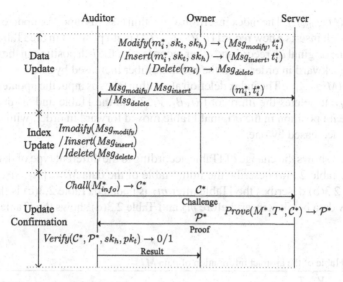

Fig. 2.3 Framework of auditing for dynamic operations

pair of data block and tag (m_i^*, t_i^*) to the server and sends the update message Msg_{modify} to the auditor.

- **Insert**$(m_i^*, sk_t, sk_h) \rightarrow (Msg_{insert}, t_i^*)$. The insertion algorithm takes as inputs the new data block m_i^*, the secret tag key sk_t and the secret hash key sk_h. It inserts a new data block m_i^* before the ith position. It generates an original number B_i^*, a new version number V_i^* and a new timestamp T_i^*. Then, it calls the TagGen to generate a new data tag t_i^* for the new data block m_i^*. It outputs the new tag t_i^* and the update message $Msg_{insert} = (i, B_i^*, V_i^*, T_i^*)$. Then, it inserts the new pair of data block and tag (m_i^*, t_i^*) on the server and sends the update message Msg_{insert} to the auditor.

- **Delete**$(m_i) \rightarrow Msg_{delete}$. The deletion algorithm takes as input the data block m_i. It outputs the update message $Msg_{delete} = (i, B_i, V_i, T_i)$. It then deletes the pair of data block and its tag (m_i, t_i) from the server and sends the update message Msg_{delete} to the auditor.

2.4.2.2 Index Update

Upon receiving the three types of update messages, the auditor calls three corresponding algorithms to update the ITable. Each algorithm is designed as follows.

- **IModify**(Msg_{modify}). The index modification algorithm takes the update message Msg_{modify} as input. It replaces the version number V_i by the new one V_i^* and modifies T_i by the new timestamp T_i^*.

- **IInsert**(Msg_{insert}). The index insertion algorithm takes as input the update message Msg_{insert}. It inserts a new record (i, B_i^*, V_i^*, T_i^*) in ith position in the ITable. It then moves the original ith record and other records after the i-th position in the previous ITable backward in order, with the index number increased by one.
- **IDelete**(Msg_{delete}). The index deletion algorithm takes as input the update message Msg_{delete}. It deletes the ith record (i, B_i, V_i, T_i) in the ITable and all the records after the ith position in the original ITable moved forward in order, with the index number decreased by one.

Table 2.3 shows the change of ITable according to the different type of data update operation. Table 2.3(a) describe the initial table of the data $M = \{m_1, m_2, \ldots, m_n\}$ and Table 2.3(b) describes the ITable after m_2 is updated. Table 2.3(c) is the ITable after a new data block is insert before m_2 and Table 2.3(d) shows the ITable after m_2 is deleted.

Table 2.3 ITable of the abstract information of data M

Index	B_i	V_i	T_i
Initial abstract information of M			
1	1	1	T_1
2	2	1	T_2
3	3	1	T_3
⋮	⋮	⋮	⋮
n	n	1	T_n
After modifying m_2, V_2 and T_2 are updated			
1	1	1	T_1
2	2	2	T_2^*
3	3	1	T_3
⋮	⋮	⋮	⋮
n	n	1	T_n
After inserting before m_2, all items before m_2 move backward with the index increased by 1			
1	1	1	T_1
2	$n+1$	1	T_{n+1}
3	2	1	T_2
⋮	⋮	⋮	⋮
$n+1$	n	1	T_n
After deleting m_2, all items after m_2 move forward with the index decreased by 1			
1	1	1	T_1
2	3	1	T_3
3	4	1	T_4
⋮	⋮	⋮	⋮
$n-1$	n	1	T_n

2.4.2.3 Update Confirmation

After the auditor updates the ITable, it conducts a confirmation auditing for the updated data and sends the result to the owner. Then, the owner can choose to delete the local version of data according to the update confirmation auditing result.

2.5 Batch Auditing for Multi-Owner and Multi-Cloud

Data storage auditing is a significant service in cloud computing which helps the owners check the data integrity on the cloud servers. Due to the large number of data owners, the auditor may receive many auditing requests from multiple data owners. In this situation, it would greatly improve the system performance, if the auditor could combine these auditing requests together and only conduct the batch auditing for multiple owners simultaneously. The previous work [31] cannot support the batch auditing for multiple owners. That is because parameters for generating the data tags used by each owner are different and thus the auditor cannot combine the data tags from multiple owners to conduct the batch auditing.

On the other hand, some data owners may store their data on more than one cloud servers. To ensure the owner's data integrity in all the clouds, the auditor will send the auditing challenges to each cloud server which hosts the owner's data, and verify all the proofs from them. To reduce the computation cost of the auditor, it is desirable to combine all these responses together and do the batch verification.

In the previous work [31], the authors proposed a cooperative provable data possession for integrity verification in multi-cloud storage. In their method, the authors apply the mask technique to ensure the data privacy, such that it requires an additional trusted organizer to send a commitment to the auditor during the commitment phase in multi-cloud batch auditing. The TSAS applies the encryption method with the Bilinearity property of the bilinear pairing to ensure the data privacy, rather than the mask technique. Thus, the multi-cloud batch auditing protocol does not have any commitment phase, such that it does not require any additional trusted organizer.

2.5.1 Algorithms for Batch Auditing for Multi-Owner and Multi-Cloud

Let O be the set of owners and S be the set of cloud servers. The batch auditing for multi-owner and multi-cloud can be constructed as follows.

2.5.1.1 Owner Initialization

Each owner $O_k (k \in O)$ runs the key generation algorithm KeyGen to generate the pair of secret-public tag key $(sk_{t,k}, pk_{t,k})$ and a set of secret hash key $\{sk_{h,kl}\}_{l \in S}$. That is, for different cloud servers, the owner has different secret hash keys. Each data component is denoted as M_{kl}, which means that this data component is owned by the owner O_k and stored on the cloud server S_l. Suppose the data component M_{kl} is divided into n_{kl} data blocks and each data block is further split into s sectors. (Here each data block is assumed to be further split into the same number of sectors. It can also use the technique proposed in Sect. 2.3.2 to deal with the situation that each data blocks is split into different number of sectors.) The owner O_k runs the tag generation algorithm TagGen to generate the data tags $T_{kl} = \{t_{kl,i}\}_{i \in [1, n_{kl}]}$ as

$$t_{kl,i} = (h(sk_{h,kl}, W_{kl,i}) \cdot \prod_{j=1}^{s} u_{k,j}^{m_{kl,ij}})^{sk_{t,k}}.$$

where $W_{kl,i} = FID_{kl}||i||B_{kl,i}||V_{kl,i}||T_{kl,i}$.

After all the data tags are generated, each owner $O_k (k \in O)$ sends the data component $M_{kl} = \{m_{kl,ij}\}_{i \in [1, n_{kl}], j \in [1, s]}^{k \in O, l \in S}$ and the data tags $T_{kl} = \{t_{kl,i}\}_{i \in [1, n_{kl}]}^{k \in O, l \in S}$ to the corresponding server S_l. Then, it sends the public tag key $pk_{t,k}$, the set of secret hash key $\{sk_{hl,k}\}_{l \in S}$, the abstract information of data $\{M_{info,kl}\}_{k \in O, l \in S}$ to the auditor.

2.5.1.2 Batch Auditing for Multi-Owner and Multi-Cloud

Let O_{chal} and S_{chal} denote the involved set of owners and cloud servers involved in the batch auditing respectively. The batch auditing also consists of three steps: Batch Challenge, Batch Proof and Batch Verification.

- **Step 1: Batch Challenge**
  During this step, the auditor runs the batch challenge algorithm BChall to generate a batch challenge $\mathcal{C}$ for a set of challenged owners O_{chal} and a set of clouds S_{chal}. The batch challenge algorithm is defined as follows.

  - **BChall**($\{M_{info,kl}\}_{k \in O, l \in S}$) $\rightarrow \mathcal{C}$. The batch challenge algorithm takes all the abstract information as input. It selects a set of owners O_{chal} and a set of cloud servers S_{chal}. For each data owner $O_k (k \in O_{chal})$, it chooses a set of data blocks as the challenged subset Q_{kl} from each server $S_l (l \in S_{chal})$. It then generates a random number $v_{kl,i}$ for each chosen data block $m_{kl,i} (k \in O_{chal}, l \in S_{chal}, i \in Q_{kl})$. It also chooses a random number $r \in \mathbb{Z}_p^*$ and computes the set of challenge stamp $\{R_k\}_{k \in O_{chal} = pk_{t,k}^r}$. It outputs the challenge as

    $$\mathcal{C} = (\{\mathcal{C}_l\}_{l \in S_{chal}}, \{R_k\}_{k \in O_{chal}}),$$

    where $\mathcal{C}_l = \{(k, l, i, v_{kl,i})\}_{k \in O_{chal}}$.

Then, the auditor sends each $\mathcal{C}_l$ to each cloud server $S_l(l \in S_{chal})$ together with the challenge stamp $\{R_k\}_{k \in O_{chal}}$.

- **Step 2: Batch Proof**

Upon receiving the challenge, each server $S_l(l \in S_{chal})$ generates a proof $\mathcal{P}_l = (TP_l, DP_l)$ by using the following batch prove algorithm BProve and sends the proof $\mathcal{P}_l$ to the auditor.

- **BProve**$(\{M_{kl}\}_{k \in O_{chal}}, \{T_{kl}\}_{k \in O_{chal}}, \mathcal{C}_l, \{R_k\}_{k \in O_{chal}}) \rightarrow \mathcal{P}_l$. The batch prove algorithm takes as inputs the data $\{M_{kl}\}_{k \in O_{chal}}$, the data tags $\{T_{kl}\}_{k \in O_{chal}}$, the received challenge $\mathcal{C}_l$ and the challenge stamp $\{R_k\}_{k \in O_{chal}}$. It generates the *tag proof* TP_l as

$$TP_l = \prod_{k \in O_{chal}} \prod_{i \in Q_{kl}} t_{kl,i}^{v_{kl,i}}.$$

Then, for each $j \in [1, s]$, it computes the sector linear combination $MP_{kl,j}$ of all the chosen data blocks of each owner $O_k(k \in O_{chal})$ as

$$MP_{kl,j} = \sum_{i \in Q_{kl}} v_{kl,i} \cdot m_{kl,ij},$$

and generates the *data proof* DP_l as

$$DP_l = \prod_{j=1}^{s} \prod_{k \in O_{chal}} e(u_{k,j}, R_k)^{MP_{kl,j}}.$$

It outputs the proof $\mathcal{P}_l = (TP_l, DP_l)$.

- **Step 3: Batch Verification**

Upon receiving all the proofs from the challenged servers, the auditor runs the following batch verification algorithm BVerify to check the correctness of the proofs.

- **BVerify**$(\mathcal{C}, \{\mathcal{P}_l\}, \{sk_{h,lk}\}, \{pk_{t,k}\}, \{M_{info,kl}\}) \rightarrow 0/1$. The batch verification algorithm takes as inputs the challenge $\mathcal{C}$, the proofs $\{\mathcal{P}_l\}_{l \in S_{chal}}$, the set of secret hash keys $\{sk_{h,kl}\}_{k \in O_{chal}, l \in S_{chal}}$, the public tag keys $\{pk_{t,k}\}_{k \in O_{chal}}$ and the abstract information of the challenged data blocks $\{M_{info,kl}\}_{k \in O_{chal}, l \in S_{chal}}$. For each owner $O_k(k \in O_{chal})$, it computes the set of identifier hash values $\{h(sk_{h,kl}, W_{kl,i})\}_{l \in S_{chal}, i \in Q_{kl}}$ for all the chosen data blocks from each challenged server, and use these hash values to compute a *challenge hash* $H_{chal,k}$ as

$$H_{chal,k} = \prod_{l \in S_{chal}} \prod_{i \in Q_{kl}} h(sk_{h,kl}, W_{kl,i})^{r v_{kl,i}}.$$

When finished the calculation of all the data owners' challenge hash $\{H_{chal,k}\}_{k \in O_{chal}}$, it verifies the proofs by the batch verification equation as

$$\prod_{l \in S_{chal}} DP_l = \frac{e(\prod_{l \in S_{chal}} TP_l, g_2^r)}{\prod_{k \in O_{chal}} e(H_{chal,k}, pk_{t,k})}. \tag{2.3}$$

If Eq. 2.3 is true, it outputs 1. Otherwise, it outputs 0.

2.5.2 Correctness Proof

The correctness of the batch auditing protocol is concluded as the following theorem:

Theorem 2.2 *In the multi-owner multi-cloud batch auditing protocol, all the challenged servers pass the audit iff all the chosen data blocks and the data tags from all the owners are correctly stored.*

Proof If the data blocks and the data tags from all the owners are stored correctly on the challenged servers, the right part of the batch verification equation can be rewritten as

$$\frac{e(\prod_{l \in S_{chal}} TP_l, g_2^r)}{\prod_{k \in O_{chal}} e(H_{chal,k}, pk_{t,k})} \tag{2.4}$$

$$= \prod_{k \in O_{chal}} \prod_{l \in S_{chal}} \prod_{i \in Q_{kl}} \frac{e(t_{kl,i}^{v_{kl,i}}, g_2^r)}{e(h(sk_{h,kl}, W_{kl,i})^{rv_{kl,i}}, pk_{t,k})}$$

$$= \prod_{k \in O_{chal}} \prod_{l \in S_{chal}} \prod_{i \in Q_{kl}} \frac{e((h(sk_{h,kl}, W_{kl,i}) \cdot \prod_{j=1}^{s} u_{k,j}^{m_{kl,ij}})^{sk_{t,k}v_{kl,i}}, g_2^r)}{e(h(sk_{h,kl}, W_{kl,i})^{v_{kl,i}sk_{t,k}}, g_2^r)}$$

$$= \prod_{l \in S_{chal}} \prod_{j=1}^{s} \prod_{k \in O_{chal}} e(u_{k,j}^{\sum_{i \in Q_{kl}} v_{kl,i}m_{kl,ij}}, pk_{t,k}^r)$$

$$= \prod_{l \in S_{chal}} \prod_{j=1}^{s} \prod_{k \in O_{chal}} e(u_{k,j}, pk_{t,k}^r)^{MP_{kl,j}}$$

$$= \prod_{l \in S_{chal}} DP_l$$

It shows that the batch verification equation can hold, if all the data blocks and tags are correctly stored on the challenged servers. Otherwise, the batch verification Eq. 2.4 does not hold. That is, the server fail to pass the audit, if any of the chosen data block or data tag is corrupted or modified.

2.6 Security Analysis

In this section, we first prove that the auditing protocols are provably secure under the security model. Then, we prove that the auditing protocols can also guarantee the data privacy. Finally, we prove that the auditing system is an interactive proof system.

2.6.1 Provably Secure Under the Security Model

The security proofs of the dynamic auditing protocol and batch auditing protocol are similar. Here, we only demonstrate the security proof for the dynamic auditing protocol, as concluded in the following theorems.

Theorem 2.3 *The dynamic auditing protocol can resist the Replace Attack from the server.*

Proof If any of the challenged data blocks m_l or its data tag t_l is corrupted or not up-to-date on the server, the server cannot pass the auditing because the verification equation cannot hold. The server may conduct the replace attack to try to pass the audit. It uses another pair of data block and data tag (m_k, t_k) to replace the chosen one (m_l, t_l). Then, the *data proof DP^** becomes

$$DP^* = \prod_{j=1}^{s} e(u_j, R)^{MP_j^*},$$

where each MP_j^* can be expressed as

$$MP_j^* = v_l \cdot m_{kj} + \sum_{i \in Q, i \neq l} v_i \cdot m_{ij}.$$

The *tag proof TP^** can be calculated as

$$TP^* = t_k^{v_l} \cdot \prod_{i \in Q, i \neq l} t_i^{v_i}.$$

Then, the left hand of the verification equation can be transformed to

$$DP^* \cdot e(H_{chal}, pk_t) = e\left(\left(\frac{h(sk_h, W_l)}{h(sk_h, W_k)}\right)^{v_l sk_t} \cdot TP^*, g_2^r\right). \tag{2.5}$$

Due to the collision resistance of hash function, $h(sk_h, W_l)/h(sk_h, W_k)$ cannot be equal to 1 in the random oracle model and thus the verification equation does not hold, such that the proof from the server cannot pass the auditing. Therefore, the dynamic auditing protocol can resist the replace attack.   □

Theorem 2.4 *The dynamic auditing protocol can resist the Forge Attack.*

Proof The server can forge the tag without knowing the secret tag key and the secret hash key, when the same hash value and the secret tag key are used for two times. For example, suppose the same hash value $h(sk_h, i)$ and the secret tag key sk_t are used for generating the data tags for two different data blocks m_i and m'_i. The two tags can be expressed as $t_i = (h(sk_h, i) \cdot g^{m_i})^{sk_t}$ and $t'_i = (h(sk_h, i) \cdot g^{m'_i})^{sk_t}$. The server can first compute

$$t_i \cdot t_i'^{-1} = g^{(m_i - m'_i)sk_t}$$

and get

$$g^{sk_t} = (t_i \cdot t_i'^{-1})^{\frac{1}{m_i - m'_i}}$$

by using the Euclidean algorithm $gcd(m_i - m'_i, p)$. Then, for any pair of data block and tag (m_k, t_k), the server can easily compute

$$h(sk_h, k)^{sk_t} = \frac{t_k}{(g^{sk_t})^{m_k}}.$$

Therefore, for any data block m^*_k, the server can forge its tag t^*_k by

$$t^*_k = t_k \cdot (t_i \cdot t_i'^{-1})^{\frac{m^*_k - m_k}{m_i - m'_i}}.$$

The above equation shows that if the same value and the secret tag key is reused for two times, the server can forge the tag and deceive the auditor.

In the dynamic auditing protocol, the server cannot forge the tags and pass the audit successfully. That is because there is no chance to get the same hash value from the abstract information of data blocks in the dynamic auditing protocol. For each data block m_i, the abstract information contains the original block number B_i, the version number V_i and the timestamp T_i. Due to the different value of timestamp T_i for each data block, it is impossible for a hash function to get two same hash values from different abstract information in the random oracle model.   □

Theorem 2.5 *The dynamic auditing protocol can resist the Replay Attack.*

Proof On one hand, in the dynamic auditing protocol, there is a challenge stamp R in each challenge-response auditing process. Because different audit processes have different challenge stamps, the server cannot only use the previous proof $\mathcal{P}$ to generate the new proof and pass the auditing without retrieving the challenged data blocks and data tags.

On the other hand, in the dynamic auditing protocol, a timestamp is introduced in the ITable, which is used to generating the tags. For different version of data blocks or new inserted data blocks, the timestamps used to generate the data tags are different. The update operations will not allow the server to launch the replay attack based on the same hash values of the abstract information. □

2.6.2 Privacy-Preserving Guarantee

The data privacy is an important requirement in the design of auditing protocol in cloud storage systems. The proposed auditing protocols are privacy-preserving as stated in the follow theorem.

Theorem 2.6 *In the proposed auditing protocols, neither the server nor the auditor can obtain any information about the data and the secret tag key during the auditing procedure.*

Proof Because the data are encrypted by owners, it is obvious that the server cannot decrypt the data without the owners' secret key. The secret hash key and the secret tag key are kept secret to the server and the server cannot deduce them based on the received information during the auditing procedure. Therefore, the data and the secret tag key are confidential against the server in the auditing protocols.

On the auditor side, it can only get the product of all the challenged data tags from the *tag proof TP*. The *data proof* in the auditing protocol is in an encrypted way by the exponentiate on the challenge stamps R. It is a discrete logarithm problem to get the linear combinations of the chosen data sectors $\{MP_j\}_{j\in[1,s]}$ from the *data proof DP*, which is similar to obtain the secret tag key sk_t from g^{sk_t}. Hence, the auditor cannot get any information about the data and the secret tag key from the proof generated by the server in the auditing protocol. For the dynamical index update, the index update messages do not contain any information about the secret tag key and the content of the data, and thus the auditor cannot obtain any information about the data content from the dynamic operations. □

2.6.3 Proof of the Interactive Proof System

In this section, we first recall the definition of the interactive proof system and the zero-knowledge in [10] as follows.

Definition 2.3 A system is a zero-knowledge interactive system if the completeness, soundness and zero-knowledge hold.

Then, we prove that the dynamic auditing system is an Interactive Proof system, which provides zero-knowledge proof to ensure both the data integrity and the data confidentiality in the cloud.

Theorem 2.7 *The storage auditing system is a zero-knowledge interactive proof system under the CBDH assumption in random oracle model.*

Proof First, we prove that the TSAS system is an interactive proof system. According to the definition of an interactive proof system in [10], an interactive proof system should satisfy the following two features:

1. *Completeness* The storage auditing scheme is complete if the verification algorithm accepts the response when the server returns a valid response. This can be proved as the correctness proof in Theorem 2.1 and Theorem 2.2.
2. *Soundness* The storage auditing scheme is sound if any cheating server that convinces the auditor that it is storing a file is actually storing that file. In other words, the server cannot conduct the forge attack successfully, which is proved by Theorem 2.4..

Then, we prove that the TSAS is zero-knowledge as follows.
Zero-knowledge Proof The only information can be revealed in each auditing procedure is the data proof *DP* and the tag proof *TP*. We construct a simulator *S* that is not interacted with the protocol $\mathcal{A}$ as follows.

Given the public tag key pk_t, the public parameter g_2 and the challenge hash H_{chal}, the simulator chooses a random $TP \in \mathbb{G}_1$ as the tag proof and a random number $r \in \mathbb{Z}_p$, then the data proof *DP* can be simulated as

$$DP = \frac{e(TP, g_2^r)}{e(H_{chal}, pk_t)} \in G_T. \tag{2.6}$$

Such randomly generated pair of (TP, DP) are computationally indistinguishable from the pair of proof generated according to the auditing protocol. Thus, the auditing protocol $\mathcal{A}$ is a zero-knowledge protocol. This completes the proof of the theorem.   □

2.7 Performance Analysis

Storage auditing is a very resource demanding service in terms of computational resource, communication cost and memory space. In this section, we give the communication cost comparison and computation complexity comparison between the TSAS and two existing works: the Audit protocol proposed by Wang et al. [26, 27] and the IPDP proposed by Zhu et al. [31, 32].

Table 2.4 Storage overhead comparison for $|M|$-bit data

Scheme	Server	Auditor
Wang's audit [26, 27]	$3 \cdot |M|$	$O(1)$
Zhu's IPDP [31, 32]	$|M|/s$	$O(1)$
TSAS	$|M|/s$	$O(1)$

s number of sectors in each data block

2.7.1 Storage Overhead

We compare the storage overhead on both the server and the auditor as described in Table 2.4.

2.7.1.1 Storage Overhead on the Server

The storage overhead on the server mainly comes from the storage of data tags. Suppose the size of data component is $|M|$ and the security parameter is set to 160-bit.

In Wang's auditing scheme, the data is divided into data blocks, and for each data block, there is a data tag. Due to the security reason, the size of each data element (in Wang's scheme, the data element is the data block) should not be larger than the security parameter. In that case, the total size of data tags should be $|M|$-bit, which is the same as the total size of data blocks. Moreover, in Wang's scheme, the server should store a MHT for the dynamic auditing, which incurs $2|M|$-bit storage overhead. Thus, in Wang's auditing scheme, the storage overhead on the server should be $3|M|$-bit, three times of the data size.

Both the TSAS and Zhu's IPDP apply the data fragment technique to further split each data block into s sectors. Since the data element is the sector in the TSAS and Zhu's IPDP, the size of each sector is corresponding to the security parameter. Then, for each data block that consists of s sectors only one data tag is generated, such that a $|M|$-bit data component only incurs $\frac{|M|}{s}$-bit storage overhead, which can greatly reduce the storage overhead.

2.7.1.2 Storage Overhead on the Auditor

The abstract information of the data contributes the main storage overhead on the auditor. In Wang's auditing scheme, the abstract data information only contains the file name, the number of data blocks. Besides the file name and the number of data blocks, in the TSAS and Zhu's IPDP, the abstract data information also includes the index table. However, the value of each item in the index table is only the number from 1 to the total number of data blocks n. The size of each item in the index table is very small compared to the data tags. For example, suppose the security parameter is 160-bit, and the number of sectors in each data block is set to 50. Then, for 10 MB data component, the number of data block is 1000, which means that TSAS can use 10 bits to describe all the values in the index table. Thus, the size of index table is 500 Bytes, which is 0.005 % of the data size. Therefore, the storage overhead on the auditor is $O(1)$.

2.7.2 Communication Cost

Because the communication cost during the initialization is almost the same in these three auditing protocols, we only compare the communication cost between the auditor and the server, which consists of the challenge and the proof.

Consider a batch auditing with K owners and C cloud servers. Suppose the number of challenged data block from each owner on different cloud servers is the same, denoted as t, and the data block are split into s sectors in Zhu's IPDP and TSAS. We do the comparison under the same probability of detection. That is, in Wang's scheme, the number of data blocks from each owner on each cloud server should be st. The result is described in Table 2.5.

From the table, we can see that the communication cost in Wang's auditing scheme is not only linear to C, K, t, s, but also linear to the total number of data blocks n. As we know, in large scale cloud storage systems, the total number of data blocks could be very large. Therefore, Wang's auditing scheme may incur high communication cost.

TSAS and Zhu's IPDP have the same total communication cost during the challenge phase. During the proof phase, the communication cost of the proof in TSAS is only linear to C, but in Zhu's IPDP, the communication cost of the proof is not only linear to C and K, but also linear to s. That is because Zhu's IPDP uses the mask technique to protect the data privacy, which requires to send both the masked proof and the encrypted mask to the auditor. In TSAS, the server is only required to send the encrypted proof to the auditor and thus incurs less communication cost than Zhu's IPDP.

Table 2.5 Communication cost comparison of batch auditing for K owners and C clouds

Scheme	Challenge	Proof
Wang's audit [26, 27]	$O(KCst)$	$O(KCst \log n)$
Zhu's IPDP [31, 32]	$O(KCt)$	$O(KCs)$
TSAS	$O(KCt)$	$O(C)$

t is the number of challenged data blocks from each owner on each cloud server
s is the number of sectors in each data block
n is the total number of data blocks of a file in Wang's scheme

2.7.3 Computation Complexity

The simulation of the computation on the owner, the server and the auditor is conducted on a Linux system with an Intel Core 2 Duo CPU at 3.16 GHz and 4.00 GB RAM. The code uses the Pairing-Based Cryptography (PBC) library version 0.5.12 to simulate TSAS and Zhu's IPDP (Under the same detection of probability, Wang's scheme requires much more data blocks than TSAS and Zhu's IPDP, such that the computation time is almost s times more than TSAS and Zhu's IPDP and thus it is not comparable). The elliptic curve used is a MNT d159-curve, where the base field size is 159-bit and the embedding degree is 6. The d159-curve has a 160-bit group order, which means p is a 160-bit length prime. All the simulation results are the mean of 20 trials.

2.7.3.1 Computation Cost of the Auditor

We compare the computation time of the auditor versus the number of data blocks, the number of clouds and the number of owners in Fig. 2.4.

Figure 2.4a shows the computation time of the auditor versus the number of challenged data blocks in the single cloud and single owner case. In this figure, the number of data blocks goes to 500 (i.e. the challenged data size equals to 500 KByte), but it can illustrate the linear relationship between the computation cost of the auditor versus the challenged data size. From the Fig. 2.4a, we can see that TSAS incurs less computation cost of the auditor than Zhu's IPDP, when coping with large number of challenged data blocks.

In real cloud storage systems, the data size is very large (e.g. petabytes), TSAS applies the sampling auditing method to ensure the integrity of such large data. The sample size and the frequency are determined by the service level agreement. From the simulation results, it requires approximate 800 s to audit for 1 GByte data. However, the computing abilities of the cloud server and the auditor are much more powerful than the simulation PC, so the computation time can be relatively small. Therefore, TSAS is practical in large scale cloud storage systems.

Figure 2.4b describes the computation cost of the auditor of the multi-cloud batch auditing scheme versus the number of challenged clouds. It is easy to find that TSAS incurs less computation cost of the auditor than Zhu's IPDP, especially when there are a large number of clouds in the large scale cloud storage systems.

Because Zhu's IPDP does not support the batch auditing for multiple owners, the simulation repeats the computation for several times which is equal to the number of data owners. Figure 2.4c compares the computation cost of the auditor between the multi-owner batch auditing and the general auditing protocol which does not support the multi-owner batch auditing (e.g. Zhu's IPDP). Figure 2.4c also demonstrates that the batch auditing for multiple owners can greatly reduce the computation cost. Although in the simulation the number of data owners goes to 500, it can illustrate the trend of computation cost of the auditor that TSAS is much more efficient than

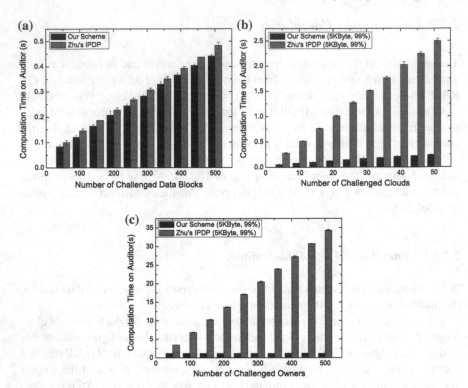

Fig. 2.4 Comparison of computation cost of the auditor (s = 50). **a** Single owner, single cloud.
b Single owner, 5 blocks/cloud. **c** Single cloud, 5 blocks/owner

Zhu's IPDP in large scale cloud storage systems that may have millions to billions
of data owners.

2.7.3.2 Computation Cost of the Server

We compare the computation cost of the server versus the number of data blocks in
Fig. 2.5a and the number of data owners in Fig. 2.5b. TSAS moves the computing
loads of the auditing from the auditor to the server, such that it can greatly reduce
the computation cost of the auditor.

2.7.4 Computation Cost of the Owner

Both TSAS and Zhu's IPDP apply the data fragment technique to reduce the number
of data blocks by further splitting data block into sectors. The number of sectors in
each data block should be carefully selected. As we mentioned, due to the security

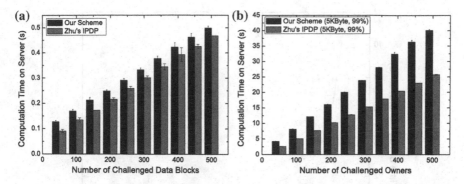

Fig. 2.5 Comparison of computation cost on the server (s = 50). **a** Single owner, single cloud. **b** Single cloud, 5 blocks/owner

reason, the size of the data element should not be larger than the security parameter. In TSAS and Zhu's IPDP, the data element is the data sector, thus the size of each data sector is fixed according to the security parameter. For a constant size data component M, the number of data blocks can be calculated as $n = \frac{sizeof(M)}{s \cdot \log p}$, where s is the number of sectors in the data block and p is the security parameter.

When considering the time of generating a tag for one data block, it is easy to see that the computation time is linear to the number of sectors in the data block. Specifically, let **Exp.** and **Mul.** be an exponentiation computation and a multiplication computation in the group respectively. Let the **H.** be the hash computation. The time of generating a data tag for one data block can be described as

$$Time_{tag}(s) = s \cdot (\textbf{Exp.} + \textbf{Mul.}) + \textbf{Exp.} + \textbf{H.}$$

The total tag generation time for a constant size of data M can be calculated as

$$TTime_{tag}(s) = \frac{sizeof(M)}{\log p} \left(\textbf{Exp.} + \textbf{Mul.} + \frac{1}{s}(\textbf{Exp.} + \textbf{H.}) \right).$$

It is easy to find that the total tag generation time for a constant size of data is linear to $\frac{1}{s}$. Figure 2.6 shows the total computation time of generating all the data tags for 1 MByte data component versus the number of sectors in each data block. We can see that for the fixed size data, when the number of sectors in a data block is increased, the total time of tag generation goes stable.

2.8 Related Work

Juels et al. proposed a Proofs Of Retrievability (POR) scheme which enables a server (prover) to give a concise proof that a user (verifier) can retrieve a target file [12]. Their POR protocol encrypts the file F and randomly embeds a set of randomly-valued

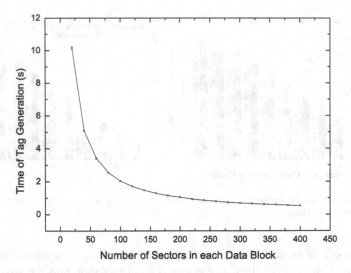

Fig. 2.6 Computation time of tag generation for 1 MByte data

check blocks called *sentinels*. The verifier challenges the prover by specifying the positions of a collection of *sentinels* and asking the prover to return the associated *sentinel* values. If the prover has modified or deleted a substantial portion of F, then it also has suppressed some *sentinels* with high probability and thus it cannot respond correctly to the verifier. The security of this protocol is proved by Dodis et al. in [7] without making any simplifying assumptions on the behavior of the adversary. However, this POR protocol is inappropriate for the proposed problem because it only allows a limited number of auditing times which is related to the number of *sentinels*.

To ensure the data integrity in remote servers, in [22, 23], the owner pre-computes some MACs of the data with different secret keys and sends all the MACs and keys to the auditor. When verifying data integrity, the auditor selects and sends a key k to the server. Then, the server computes the MAC with k and returns it to the auditor for comparison with the one stored on it. However, the number of times a particular data item can be verified is limited by the number of secret keys that fixed beforehand. Besides, the auditor needs to store several MACs for each file. Therefore, Shah's auditing protocols still cannot be applied to the problem.

Filho et al. [9] proposed a cryptographic protocol based on RSA-based secure hash function, through which a prover can demonstrate possession of a set of data known to the verifier. But in their protocol the prover needs to exponentiate the entire data file which will cause high computation cost. To overcome the drawback of Filho's protocol, Sebe et al. [20] improved the protocol by first dividing data into blocks and fingerprinting each block and then using a RSA-based hash function on each block. Then, a Diffie-Hellman-based approach is used to verify the data integrity. Their protocol can reduce the computation time of verification by trading off the computation time required at the prover against the storage required at the verifier.

Similarly, Yamamoto et al. [28] proposed a fast integrity checking scheme through batch verification of homomorphic hash functions on randomly selected blocks of data. However, in their schemes, the verifier needs to store a copy of the meta-data, such that they cannot be applied to the storage auditing in cloud storage system.

Ateniese et al. proposed a Sampling Provable Data Possession (SPDP) scheme [2], which combines the RSA cryptography with Homomorphic Verifiable Tags (HVT). It divides the data into several data blocks and encrypts each data block. For each auditing query, the auditor only challenge a subset of data blocks. By using such sampling method, the integrity of entire data can be guaranteed, when sufficient number of such sampling auditing queries are conducted. This sampling mechanism is applied in many remote integrity checking scheme, because it could significantly reduce the workloads of the server. Although the SPDP scheme can keep the data privacy, it cannot support the dynamic auditing and the batch auditing for multiple owners.

To support the dynamic auditing, Ateniese et al. developed a dynamic provable data possession protocol [3] based on cryptographic hash function and symmetric key encryption. Their idea is to pre-compute a certain number of metadata during the setup period, so that the number of updates and challenges is limited and fixed beforehand. In their protocol, each update operation requires recreating all the remaining metadata, which is problematic for large files. Moreover, their protocol cannot perform block insertions anywhere (only append-type insertions are allowed). Erway et al. [8] also extended the PDP model to support dynamic updates on the stored data and proposed two dynamic provable data possession scheme by using a new version of authenticated dictionaries based on rank information. However, their schemes may cause heavy computation burden to the server since they relied on the PDP scheme proposed by the Ateniese.

In [27], the authors proposed a dynamic auditing protocol that can support the dynamic operations of the data on the cloud servers, but this method may leak the data content to the auditor because it requires the server to send the linear combinations of data blocks to the auditor. In [26], the authors extended their dynamic auditing scheme to be privacy-preserving and support the batch auditing for multiple owners. However, due to the large number of data tags, their auditing protocols will incur a heavy storage overhead on the server. In [31], Zhu et al. proposed a cooperative provable data possession scheme that can support the batch auditing for multiple clouds and also extend it to support the dynamic auditing in [32]. However, it is impossible for their scheme to support the batch auditing for multiple owners. That is because parameters for generating the data tags used by each owner are different and thus they cannot combine the data tags from multiple owners to conduct the batch auditing. Another drawback is that their scheme requires an additional trusted organizer to send a commitment to the auditor during the batch auditing for multiple clouds, because their scheme applies the mask technique to ensure the data privacy. However, such additional organizer is not practical in cloud storage systems. Furthermore, both Wang's schemes and Zhu's schemes incur heavy computation cost of the auditor, which makes the auditing system inefficient.

2.9 Conclusion

In this chapter, we introduced TSAS, an efficient and inherently secure dynamic auditing protocol. It protects the data privacy against the auditor by combining the cryptography method with the bilinearity property of bilinear paring, rather than using the mask technique. Thus, the multi-cloud batch auditing protocol in TSAS does not require any additional organizer. The batch auditing protocol in TSAS can also support the batch auditing for multiple owners. Furthermore, TSAS incurs less communication cost and less computation cost of the auditor by moving the computing loads of auditing from the auditor to the server, which greatly improves the auditing performance and can be applied to large scale cloud storage systems.

References

1. Armbrust, M., Fox, A., Griffith, R., Joseph, A.D., Katz, R.H., Konwinski, A., Lee, G., Patterson, D.A., Rabkin, A., Stoica, I., Zaharia, M.: A view of cloud computing. Commun. ACM **53**(4), 50–58 (2010)
2. Ateniese, G., Burns, R.C., Curtmola, R., Herring, J., Kissner, L., Peterson, Z.N.J., Song, D.X.: Provable data possession at untrusted stores. In: Proceedings of the 14th ACM conference on computer and communications security (CCS'07), pp. 598–609. ACM (2007)
3. Ateniese, G., Di Pietro, R., Mancini, L.V., Tsudik, G.: Scalable and efficient provable data possession. In: Proceedings of the 4th international conference on Security and privacy in communication networks (SecureComm'08), pp. 1–10. ACM (2008)
4. Ateniese, G., Kamara, S., Katz, J.: Proofs of storage from homomorphic identification protocols. In: Proceedings of the 15th international conference on the theory and application of cryptology and information security: advances in cryptology—ASIACRYPT'09, pp. 319–333. Springer (2009)
5. Bairavasundaram, L.N., Goodson, G.R., Pasupathy, S., Schindler, J.: An analysis of latent sector errors in disk drives. In: Proceedings of the 2007 ACM SIGMETRICS International conference on measurement and modeling of computer systems (SIGMETRICS'07), pp. 289–300. ACM (2007)
6. Deswarte, Y., Quisquater, J., Saidane, A.: Remote integrity checking. In: The sixth working conference on integrity and internal control in information systems (IICIS). Springer, Netherlands (2004)
7. Dodis, Y., Vadhan, S.P., Wichs, D.: Proofs of retrievability via hardness amplification. In: Proceedings of the 6th theory of cryptography conference (TCC'09), pp. 109–127. Springer (2009)
8. Erway, C.C., Küpçü, A., Papamanthou, C., Tamassia, R.: Dynamic provable data possession. In: Proceedings of the 16th ACM conference on computer and communications security (CCS'09), pp. 213–222. ACM (2009)
9. Filho, D.L.G., Barreto, P.S.L.M.: Demonstrating data possession and uncheatable data transfer. IACR Cryptology ePrint Archive **2006**, 150 (2006)
10. Goldreich, O.: Zero-knowledge twenty years after its invention. Electron. Colloquium Comput. Complex. **63** (2002)
11. Goodson, G.R., Wylie, J.J., Ganger, G.R., Reiter, M.K.: Efficient byzantine-tolerant erasure-coded storage. In: Proceedings of the 2004 international conference on dependable systems and networks (DSN'04), pp. 135–144. IEEE Computer Society (2004)
12. Juels, A., Jr., Kaliski, B.S.: PORS: proofs of retrievability for large files. In: Proceedings of the 14th ACM conference on computer and communications security (CCS'07), pp. 584–597. ACM (2007)

13. Kher, V., Kim, Y.: Securing distributed storage: challenges, techniques, and systems. In: Proceedings of the 2005 ACM workshop on storage security and survivability (StorageSS05), pp. 9–25. ACM (2005)
14. Li, J., Krohn, M.N., Mazières, D., Shasha, D.: Secure untrusted data repository (sundr). In: Proceedings of the 6th conference on symposium on operating systems design and implementation, pp. 121–136. Berkeley, CA, USA (2004)
15. Lillibridge, M., Elnikety, S., Birrell, A., Burrows, M., Isard, M.: A cooperative internet backup scheme. In: Proceedings of the general track: 2003 USENIX annual technical conference, pp. 29–41. USENIX (2003)
16. Mell, P., Grance, T.: The NIST definition of cloud computing. Tech. report, National Institute of Standards and Technology (2009)
17. Naor, M., Rothblum, G.N.: The complexity of online memory checking. J. ACM 56(1), 1–46 (2009)
18. Schroeder, B., Gibson, G.A.: Disk failures in the real world: What does an mttf of 1, 000, 000 hours mean to you. In: Proceedings of the 5th USENIX conference on file and storage technologies (FAST'07), pp. 1–16. USENIX (2007)
19. Schwarz, T.J.E., Miller, E.L.: Store, forget, and check: Using algebraic signatures to check remotely administered storage. In: Proceedings of the 26th IEEE international conference on distributed computing systems (ICDCS'06) (2006)
20. Sebé, F., Domingo-Ferrer, J., Martínez-Ballesté, A., Deswarte, Y., Quisquater, J.J.: Efficient remote data possession checking in critical information infrastructures. IEEE Trans. Knowl. Data Eng. 20(8), 1034–1038 (2008)
21. Shacham, H., Waters, B.: Compact proofs of retrievability. In: Proceedings of the 14th international conference on the theory and application of cryptology and information security: advances in cryptology—ASIACRYPT'08, pp. 90–107. Springer (2008)
22. Shah, M.A., Baker, M., Mogul, J.C., Swaminathan, R.: Auditing to keep online storage services honest. In: Proceedings of the 11th workshop on hot topics in operating systems (HotOS'07). USENIX Association (2007)
23. Shah, M.A., Swaminathan, R., Baker, M.: Privacy-preserving audit and extraction of digital contents. IACR Cryptology ePrint Archive 2008, 186 (2008)
24. Velte, T., Velte, A., Elsenpeter, R.: Cloud computing: a practical approach, 1 edn., chap. 7. McGraw-Hill Inc., New York (2010)
25. Wang, C., Ren, K., Lou, W., Li, J.: Toward publicly auditable secure cloud data storage services. IEEE Netw. 24(4), 19–24 (2010)
26. Wang, C., Wang, Q., Ren, K., Lou, W.: Privacy-preserving public auditing for data storage security in cloud computing. In: Proceedings of the 29th IEEE international conference on computer communications (INFOCOM'10), pp. 525–533. IEEE (2010)
27. Wang, Q., Wang, C., Ren, K., Lou, W., Li, J.: Enabling public auditability and data dynamics for storage security in cloud computing. IEEE Trans. Parallel Distrib. Syst. 22(5), 847–859 (2011)
28. Yamamoto, G., Oda, S., Aoki, K.: Fast integrity for large data. In: Proceedings of the ECRYPT workshop on software performance enhancement for encryption and decryption, pp. 21–32. ECRYPT, Amsterdam, the Netherlands (2007)
29. Yang, K., Jia, X.: Data storage auditing service in cloud computing: challenges, methods and opportunities. World Wide Web 15(4), 409–428 (2012)
30. Zeng, K.: Publicly verifiable remote data integrity. In: Proceedings of the 10th international conference on information and communications security (ICICS'08), pp. 419–434. Springer (2008)
31. Zhu, Y., Hu, H., Ahn, G., Yu, M.: Cooperative provable data possession for integrity verification in multi-cloud storage. IEEE Trans. Parallel Distrib. Syst. 23(12) 2231–2244 (2012)
32. Zhu, Y., Wang, H., Hu, Z., Ahn, G.J., Hu, H., Yau, S.S.: Dynamic audit services for integrity verification of outsourced storages in clouds. In: Proceedings of the 2011 ACM symposium on applied computing (SAC'11), pp. 1550–1557. ACM (2011)

Chapter 3
ABAC: Attribute-Based Access Control

Abstract Cloud storage service allows data owner to outsource their data to the cloud and through which provide the data access to the users. Because the cloud server and the data owner are not in the same trust domain, the semi-trusted cloud server cannot be relied to enforce the access policy. To address this challenge, traditional methods usually require the data owner to encrypt the data and deliver decryption keys to authorized users. These methods, however, normally involve complicated key management and high overhead on data owner. In this chapter, we introduce ABAC, an access control framework for cloud storage systems that achieves fine-grained access control based on an adapted Ciphertext-Policy Attribute-based Encryption (CP-ABE) approach. In ABAC, an efficient attribute revocation method is proposed to cope with the dynamic changes of users' access privileges in large-scale systems.

3.1 Introduction

Cloud storage service allows data owners to host their data in the cloud and rely on the cloud server to provide "24/7/365" data access to the users (data consumers). Because the cloud storage service separates the roles of the data owner from the data service provider, and the data owner does not interact with the user directly for providing data access service, the data access control becomes a challenging issue for cloud storage systems. Existing methods [16] usually delegate data access control to a trusted server and let it be in charge of defining and enforcing access policies. However, the cloud server cannot be fully trusted by data owners, since the cloud server may give data access to unauthorized users to make more profit (e.g., the competitor of a company). Thus, traditional server-based data access control methods are no longer suitable for cloud storage systems. This chapter studies the data access control issue in cloud storage systems, where the data owner is in charge of defining and enforcing the access policy.

K. Yang and X. Jia, *Security for Cloud Storage Systems*, SpringerBriefs
in Computer Science, DOI: 10.1007/978-1-4614-7873-7_3,
© The Author(s) 2014

The Ciphertext-Policy Attribute-based Encryption (CP-ABE) [2, 21] is regarded as one of the most suitable technologies for data access control in cloud storage systems, because it gives the data owner more direct control on access policies and the policy checking occurs "inside the cryptography". In CP-ABE scheme, there is an authority that is responsible for attribute management. Each owner in the system is associated with a set of attributes that describe its role or identity in the system. To encrypt a file, the data owner first defines an access policy over the universal attribute set, and then encrypts it under this access policy. Only the users whose attributes satisfy the access policy are able to decrypt the ciphertext. However, due to the *attribute revocation problem*, it is very costly to apply the CP-ABE approach to control the data access in cloud storage systems. To address this problem, there are two requirements:

1. *Backward Security* The revoked user (whose attribute is revoked) cannot decrypt any new published ciphertext which requires the revoked attribute to decrypt.
2. *Forward Security* The newly joined user who has sufficient attributes is still able to decrypt the ciphertexts which were published before it joined the system.

Existing attribute revocation methods proposed for CP-ABE systems usually rely on the fully trusted server, thus they cannot be applied into cloud storage systems. The attribute revocation is still an open problem in the design of attribute-based data access control schemes for cloud storage systems.

In this chapter, we study the data security issues in cloud storage systems and describe Attribute-Based Access Control (ABAC), an attribute-based data access control scheme, where the server is not required to be fully trusted and data owners are not required to be online all the time. In ABAC, the access policy is defined and enforced by data owners rather than by cloud server. The attribute revocation method in ABAC achieves both forward security and backward security, and incurs less computation cost and communication overhead. Moreover, the revocation is conducted efficiently on attribute level rather than on user level.

3.2 Preliminary

We give some formal definitions for access structures, Linear Secret Sharing Schemes (LSSS) and the background information on Bilinear Pairings.

3.2.1 Access Structures

Definition 3.1 (**Access Structure**) Let $\{P_1, P_2, \ldots, P_n\}$ be a set of parties. A collection $\mathbb{A} \subseteq 2^{\{P_1, P_2, \ldots, P_n\}}$ is monotone if $\forall B, C$ if $B \in \mathbb{A}$ and $B \subseteq C$ then $C \in \mathbb{A}$. An access structure (respectively, monotone access structure) is a collection (respectively, monotone collection) $\mathbb{A}$ of non-empty subsets of $\{P_1, P_2, \ldots, P_n\}$, i.e., $\mathbb{A} \subseteq 2^{\{P_1, P_2, \ldots, P_n\}} \setminus \{\varnothing\}$. The sets in $\mathbb{A}$ are called the authorized sets, and the sets not in $\mathbb{A}$ are called the unauthorized sets.

In ABAC, the role of the parties is taken by the attributes. Thus, the access structure $\mathbb{A}$ will contain the authorized sets of attributes. We restrict our attention to monotone access structures. From now on, unless stated otherwise, by an access structure we mean a monotone access structure.

3.2.2 Linear Secret Sharing Schemes

The Linear Secret Sharing Schemes (LSSS) is defined as

Definition 3.2 (Linear Secret-Sharing Schemes (LSSS)) A secret-sharing scheme Π over a set of parties $\mathcal{P}$ is called linear (over $\mathbb{Z}_p$) if

1. The shares for each party form a vector over $\mathbb{Z}_p$.
2. There exists a matrix M called the share-generating matrix for Π. The matrix M has l rows and n columns. For all $i = 1, \ldots, l$, the i-th row of M is labeled by a party $\rho(i)$ (ρ is a function from $\{1, \ldots, l\}$ to $\mathcal{P}$). When we consider the column vector $v = (s, r_2, \ldots, r_n)$, where $s \in \mathbb{Z}_p$ is the secret to be shared and $r_2, \ldots, r_n \in \mathbb{Z}_p$ are randomly chosen, then Mv is the vector of l shares of the secret s according to Π. The share $(Mv)_i$ belongs to party $\rho(i)$.

Every linear secret sharing-scheme according to the above definition also enjoys the *linear reconstruction* property: Suppose that Π is a LSSS for the access structure $\mathbb{A}$. Let $S \in \mathbb{A}$ be any authorized set, and let $I \subset \{1, 2, \ldots, l\}$ be defined as $I = \{i : \rho(i) \in S\}$. Then, there exist constants $\{w \in \mathbb{Z}_p\}_{i \in I}$ such that, for any valid shares $\{\lambda_i\}$ of a secret s according to Π, we have $\sum_{i \in I} w_i \lambda_i = s$. These constants $\{w_i\}$ can be found in time polynomial in the size of the share-generating matrix M. Note that for unauthorized sets, no such constants $\{w_i\}$ exist.

3.2.3 Bilinear Pairing

Let $\mathbb{G}_1$, $\mathbb{G}_2$ and $\mathbb{G}_T$ be three multiplicative groups with the same prime order p. A bilinear map is a map $e : \mathbb{G}_1 \times \mathbb{G}_2 \to \mathbb{G}_T$ with the following properties:

1. Bilinearity: $e(u^a, v^b) = e(u, v)^{ab}$ for all $u \in \mathbb{G}_1$, $v \in \mathbb{G}_2$ and $a, b \in \mathbb{Z}_p$.
2. Non-degeneracy: There exist $u \in \mathbb{G}_1$, $v \in \mathbb{G}_2$ such that $e(u, v) \neq I$, where I is the identity element of $\mathbb{G}_T$.
3. Computability: e can be computed in an efficient way.

Such a bilinear map is called a bilinear pairing. If g_1 and g_2 are the generators of $\mathbb{G}_1$ and $\mathbb{G}_2$ respectively, $e(g_1, g_2)$ is the generator of $\mathbb{G}_T$. The bilinear pairing applied in ABAC is symmetric, where $\mathbb{G}_1 = \mathbb{G}_2 = \mathbb{G}$.

3.2.4 q-Parallel BDHE Assumption

We recall the definition of the decisional q-parallel Bilinear Diffie-Hellman Exponent (q-parallel BDHE) problem in [21] as follows. Choose a group $\mathbb{G}$ of prime order p according to the security parameter. Let $a, s, b_1, \ldots, b_q \in \mathbb{Z}_p$ be chosen at random and g be a generator of $\mathbb{G}$. If an adversary is given

$$\mathbf{y} = (g, g^s, g^a, \ldots, g^{(a^q)}, g^{(a^{q+2})}, \ldots, g^{(a^{2q})}$$
$$\forall_{1 \leq j \leq q} \ g^{s \cdot b_j}, \ g^{a/b_j}, \ldots, g^{(a^q/b_j)}, g^{(a^{q+2}/b_j)}, \ldots, g^{(a^{2q}/b_j)}$$
$$\forall_{1 \leq j, k \leq q, k \neq j} \ g^{a \cdot s \cdot b_k/b_j}, \ldots, g^{(a^q \cdot s \cdot b_k/b_j)}),$$

it must be hard to distinguish a valid tuple $e(g, g)^{a^{q+1}s} \in \mathbb{G}_T$ from a random element R in $\mathbb{G}_T$.

An algorithm $\mathcal{B}$ that outputs $z \in \{0, 1\}$ has advantage ε in solving q-parallel BDHE in $\mathbb{G}$ if

$$\left| Pr[\mathcal{B}(\mathbf{y}, T = e(g, g)^{a^{q+1}s}) = 0] - Pr[\mathcal{B}(\mathbf{y}, T = R) = 0] \right| \geq \varepsilon.$$

Definition 3.3 The decisional q-parallel BDHE assumption holds if no polynomial time algorithm has a non-negligible advantage in solving the q-parallel BDHE problem.

3.3 System and Security Model

3.3.1 System Model

Figure 3.1 describes the system model of ABAC. There are four entities in the system: Authority, Data owners (owners), Cloud server (server) and Data consumers (users).

The authority is responsible for entitling/revoking/re-granting attributes to/from/to users according to their role or identity in the system. It assigns secret keys to users when they are entitled attributes and maintains a version number of each attribute. When an attribute is revoked, the authority will update the version number of the

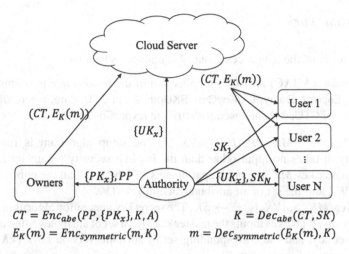

$$CT = Enc_{abe}(PP, \{PK_x\}, K, A) \qquad K = Dec_{abe}(CT, SK)$$
$$E_K(m) = Enc_{symmetric}(m, K) \qquad m = Dec_{symmetric}(E_K(m), K)$$

Fig. 3.1 System model of access control in cloud storage

revoked attribute, and generate a corresponding update key. The update key is used to update secret keys for non-revoked users[1] and the ciphertexts on the cloud servers.

The owners determine the access policies and encrypt their data under the policies before hosting them in the cloud (For simplicity, the data here means the content key[2]).

The cloud server stores the owners' data and provides data access service to users. But the server does not engage in the data access control. Instead, it is assumed that the ciphertext may be accessed by all the legal users in the system. But, the *access control happens inside the cryptography*. That is only the users who possess eligible attributes (satisfying the access policy) can decrypt the ciphertext.

Each user is entitled a set of attributes according to its roles or identity in the system. However, the user's attribute set may dynamically change due to the role changed of the user in the system. For example, when a user is degraded from the manager to the normal worker, some of its attributes should be revoked, while sometimes the revoked attribute need to be re-granted to the user. The user can decrypt the ciphertext only when he/she has sufficient attributes satisfying the access policy associated with the ciphertext.

---

[1] We use *non-revoked users* to denote those users who hold the revoked attribute but not been revoked.

[2] In practical, the data is encrypted with a content key by using symmetric encryption method, and the content key is encrypted by using CP-ABE.

3.3.2 Framework

The framework of the data access control is defined as follows.

Definition 3.4 (**ABAC**) ABAC is a collection of the following algorithms: Setup, SKeyGen, Encrypt, Decrypt, UKeyGen, SKUpdate and CTUpdate, where UKeyGen, SKUpdate and CTUpdate are used for attribute revocation.

- **Setup**$(1^\lambda) \rightarrow (MK, PP, \{PK_x\}, \{VK_x\})$. The setup algorithm is run by the authority. It takes no input other than the implicit security parameter λ. It outputs a master key MK, the public parameters PP, the set of all the public attribute keys $\{PK_x\}$ and the set of all attribute version keys $\{VK_x\}$.
- **SKeyGen**$(MK, S, \{VK_x\}_{x \in S}) \rightarrow SK$. The secret key generation algorithm is run by the authority. It takes as inputs the master key MK, a set of attributes S that describes the secret key, and the corresponding set of attribute version keys $\{VK_x\}_{x \in S}$. It outputs the user's secret key SK.
- **Encrypt**$(PP, \{PK_x\}, m, \mathbb{A}) \rightarrow CT$. The encryption algorithm is run by the data owner. It takes as inputs the public parameters PP, the set of public attribute key $\{PK_x\}$, a message m and an access structure $\mathbb{A}$ over the universe of attributes. The algorithm will encrypt m such that only a user who possesses a set of attributes satisfying the access structure will be able to decrypt the message. It outputs a ciphertext CT.
- **Decrypt**$(CT, SK) \rightarrow m$. The decryption algorithm is run by the user. It takes as inputs the ciphertext CT which contains an access structure $\mathbb{A}$ and the secret key SK for a set of attributes S. If the set of attributes S satisfies the access structure $\mathbb{A}$, then the algorithm will decrypt the ciphertext and return a message m.
- **UKeyGen**$(MK, VK_{x'}) \rightarrow (\widetilde{VK}_{x'}, UK_{x'})$. The update key generation algorithm is run by the authority. It takes as inputs the master key MK and the current version key $VK_{x'}$ of the revoked attribute x'. It outputs a new version key $\widetilde{VK}_{x'}$ of the revoked attribute x' and an update key $UK_{x'}$.
- **SKUpdate**$(MK, SK, UK_{x'}) \rightarrow \widetilde{SK}$. The secret key update algorithm is run by the authority. It takes as inputs the master key MK, the current secret key SK and the update key $UK_{x'}$ of the revoked attribute x'. It outputs a new secret key $\widetilde{SK}$.
- **CTUpdate**$(CT, UK_{x'}) \rightarrow \widetilde{CT}$. The ciphertext update algorithm is run by the cloud server. It takes as inputs the ciphertext CT and the update key $UK_{x'}$. It outputs a new ciphertext $\widetilde{CT}$.

3.3.3 Security Model

In cloud storage systems, the cloud server may give access permission to the users who are not authorized. In ABAC, the server is assumed to be curious but honest. It is curious about the content of the encrypted data or the received message, but will execute correctly the task assigned by the authority. The users, however, are assumed to be dishonest and may collude to obtain unauthorized access to data.

We now describe the security model for CP-ABE systems by the following game between a challenger and an adversary as follows.

- **Setup**. The challenger runs the Setup algorithm and gives the public parameters *PP*, and the public keys *PK* to the adversary.
- **Phase 1**. The adversary is given oracle access to secret keys *SK* that corresponding to sets of attributes $S_1, S_2, \ldots, S_{q1}$ and the update keys *UK*.
- **Challenge**. The adversary submits two equal length messages M_0 and M_1. In addition, the adversary gives a challenge access structure $\mathbb{A}^*$ such that none of the secret keys and updated keys queried from Phase 1 satisfy the access structure. The challenger flips a random coin b, and encrypts M_b under the access structure $\mathbb{A}^*$. Then, the ciphertext CT^* is given to the adversary.
- **Phase 2**. Phase 1 is repeated with the restrictions: (1) none of sets of attributes $S_{q1+1}, \ldots, S_q$ satisfy the access structure corresponding to the challenge; (2) none of the updated secret keys $\widetilde{SK}$ (generated by the queried *SK* and update keys *UK*) can decrypt the challenge ciphertext.
- **Guess**. The adversary outputs a guess b' of b.

The advantage of an adversary $\mathcal{A}$ in this game is defined as $Pr[b' = b] - 1/2$. This security model can easily be extended to handle chosen-ciphertext attacks by allowing for decryption queries in Phase 1 and Phase 2.

Definition 3.5 A revocable CP-ABE scheme is secure if all polynomial time adversaries have at most a negligible advantage in the above game.

3.4 ABAC: Attribute-Based Access Control with Efficient Revocation

In this section, we first give an overview of the method and then propose the detailed construction of access control scheme. After that, we describe the attribute revocation method to cope with the dynamic changes of users' attributes in large-scale storage systems.

3.4.1 Overview

To achieve fine-grained access control, the owner first divides the data into several components according to the logic granularities and encrypts each data component with different content keys by using symmetric encryption techniques. Then, the owner applies CP-ABE methods to encrypt each content key, such that only the user whose attributes satisfy the access structure in the ciphertext can decrypt the content keys. Users with different attributes can decrypt different number of content keys and thus obtain different granularities of information from the same data.

Since the constructions of the existing CP-ABE schemes are not suitable for attribute revocation, it is difficult to directly apply them as the underlying techniques to design the data access control scheme. Thus, ABAC first designs a new underlying CP-ABE scheme that supports attribute revocation, where each attribute is assigned with a version number. When an attribute is revoked from a user, the authority generates a new version key and an update key for this revoked attribute. With the update key, all the non-revoked users can update their secret keys (Backward Security). By using the update key, the components associated with the revoked attribute in the ciphertext can also be updated to the current version. To improve the efficiency, ABAC delegates the workload of ciphertext update to the server by using the proxy re-encryption method, such that the newly joined user is also able to decrypt the previous published data, which are encrypted with the previous public keys (Forward Security). Moreover, all the users need to hold only the latest secret key, rather than keep records on all the previous secret keys.

3.4.2 Construction of ABAC

Let $\mathbb{G}$ and $\mathbb{G}_T$ be the multiplicative groups with the same prime order p and e : $\mathbb{G} \times \mathbb{G} \to \mathbb{G}_T$ be the bilinear map. Let g be the generator of $\mathbb{G}$. Let $H : \{0, 1\}^* \to \mathbb{G}$ be a hash function such that the security will be modeled in the random oracle.

The construction of ABAC consists of four phases: *System Initialization, Key Generation by Authority, Data Encryption by Owners* and *Data Decryption by Users*.

3.4.2.1 System Initialization

The authority initializes the system by running the Setup algorithm. It randomly chooses $\alpha, \beta, \gamma, a \in \mathbb{Z}_p$ as the master key $MK = (\alpha, \beta, \gamma, a)$. Then, it generates the public parameters PP as

$$PP = (\, g, \, g^a, \, g^{1/\beta}, \, g^\beta, \, e(g, g)^\alpha \,)$$

For each attribute x, the authority generates a random number $v_x \in \mathbb{Z}_p$ as the initial attribute version number $VK_x = v_x$ and then applies it to generate a public attribute key PK_x as

$$PK_x = (\, PK_{1,x} = H(x)^{v_x}, \, PK_{2,x} = H(x)^{v_x \gamma} \,).$$

All the public parameters PP and the public attribute keys $\{PK_x\}$ are published on the public bulletin board of the authority, such that all the owners in the system can freely get them.

3.4.2.2 Secret Key Generation for Users

When a user joins the system, the authority first assigns a set of attributes S to this user according to its role or identity. Then, it generates the secret key SK for this user by running the secret key generation algorithm SKeyGen. It takes as inputs the master key MK, a set of attributes S that describes the secret key, and the corresponding set of attribute version keys $\{VK_x\}_{x \in S}$. It then chooses a random number $t \in \mathbb{Z}_p$ and generates the user's secret key as

$$SK = (\, K = g^{\frac{\alpha}{\beta}} \cdot g^{\frac{at}{\beta}}, L = g^t, \forall x \in S : K_x = g^{t\beta^2} \cdot H(x)^{v_x t \beta} \,).$$

The authority then sends SK to the user via a secure channel.

3.4.2.3 Data Encryption by Owners

Before outsourcing data M to the cloud servers, the owner processes the data as follows.

1. It first divides the data into several data components as $M = \{m_1, \ldots, m_n\}$ according to the logic granularities. For example, the person record data may be divided into {name, address, security number, employer, salary};
2. It encrypts each data component m_i with different content keys $k_i (i = 1, \ldots, n)$ by using the symmetric encryption techniques;
3. For each content key $k_i (i = 1, \ldots, n)$, the owner defines the access structure $\mathcal{M}$ over the universe of attributes $\mathbb{S}$ and then encrypts k_i under this access structure by running the encryption algorithm Encrypt.

The encryption algorithm Encrypt can be constructed as follows. It takes as inputs the public parameters PP, a set of public attribute key $\{PK_x\}$, a content key k and a LSSS access structure $(\mathcal{M}, \rho)$. Let $\mathcal{M}$ be a $l \times n$ matrix, where l denotes the number of attributes involved in the encryption. The function ρ associates rows of $\mathcal{M}$ to attributes. It first chooses a random encryption exponent $s \in \mathbb{Z}_p$ and a random vector $\mathbf{v} = (s, y_2, \ldots, y_n) \in \mathbb{Z}_p^n$, where $y_2, \ldots, y_n$ are used to share the encryption exponent s. For $i = 1$ to l, it computes $\lambda_i = \mathbf{v} \cdot \mathcal{M}_i$, where $\mathcal{M}_i$ is the vector corresponding to the i-th row of $\mathcal{M}$. Then, it randomly chooses $r_1, r_2, \ldots, r_l \in \mathbb{Z}_p$ and computes the ciphertext as

$$CT = (\, C = ke(g, g)^{\alpha s}, \ C' = g^{\beta s}, \ C_i = g^{a\lambda_i}(g^\beta)^{-r_i}H(\rho(i))^{-r_i v_{\rho(i)}},$$
$$D_{1,i} = H(\rho(i))^{v_{\rho(i)} r_i \gamma}, \ D_{2,i} = g^{\frac{r_i}{\beta}} \ (i = 1, \ldots, l) \,).$$

The owner then uploads the encrypted data to the server in the format as described in Fig. 3.2.

Fig. 3.2 Data format on cloud
server

$$\boxed{CT_1\,|\,E_{K_1}(m_1)}\;\cdots\;\boxed{}\;\cdots\;\boxed{CT_n\,|\,E_{K_n}(m_n)}$$

3.4.2.4 Data Decryption by Users

Upon receiving the data from the server, the user runs the decryption algorithm
Decrypt to obtain the corresponding content keys and uses them to further decrypt data
components. Only the attributes that the user possesses satisfy the access structure
defined in the ciphertext CT, the user can get the data component successfully. Users
with different attributes will be able to decrypt different number of data components,
such that they can get different granularities of information from the same data.

The decryption algorithm Decrypt is constructed as follows. It takes as inputs a
ciphertext CT attached with the access structure $(\mathcal{M}, \rho)$ and the secret key for a set
of attributes S. Suppose that the user's attribute set S satisfies the access structure
and let $I \subset \{1, 2, \ldots, l\}$ be defined as $I = \{i : \rho(i) \in S\}$. Then, it chooses a set of
constants $\{w_i \in \mathbb{Z}_p\}_{i \in I}$ and reconstructs the encryption exponent as $s = \sum_{i \in I} w_i \lambda_i$
if $\{\lambda_i\}$ are valid shares of the secret s according to $\mathcal{M}$. The decryption algorithm first
computes

$$
\frac{e(C', K)}{\prod_{i \in I}(e(C_i, L)e(D_{2,i}, K_{\rho(i)}))^{w_i}}
$$

$$
= \frac{e(g^{\beta s}, g^{\frac{\alpha}{\beta}} \cdot g^{\frac{at}{\beta}})}{\prod_{i \in I}(e(g^{a\lambda_i}H(\rho(i))^{-v_{\rho(i)}r_i}, g^t) \cdot e(g^{\frac{r_i}{\beta}}, H(\rho(i))^{v_{\rho(i)}t\beta}))^{w_i}} \tag{3.1}
$$

$$
= \frac{e(g, g)^{\alpha s}e(g, g)^{sat}}{e(g, g)^{at \sum_{i \in I} \lambda_i w_i}}
$$

$$
= e(g, g)^{\alpha s}
$$

It can then decrypt the content key as

$$
k = C / e(g, g)^{\alpha s}.
$$

The user then uses the content keys to further decrypt the data.

3.4.3 Attribute Revocation Method

In large-scale data storage systems, the users' access privileges may dynamically
change. For example, when a user is leaving the system, it loses the access privileges

of all the data in the cloud, which is called *User Revocation*. When a user is degraded in the system, it only loses part access privilege as some attributes should be removed from it, which is called the *Attribute Revocation*.

As we mentioned before, there are two basic requirements for the design of efficient attribute revocation methods:

1. The revoked user cannot decrypt any new published ciphertext with its previous secret key, called *Backward Security*;
2. The newly joined user who has sufficient attributes can still decrypt the ciphertexts which were published before it joined the system, called *Forward Security*. For example, in a company, an archive document is encrypted under the policy "IT department & Developer". When a new developer joins the IT department of this company, he/she should also be able to decrypt the archive document.

In order to satisfy the requirements of attribute revocation, the revocation method includes three phases: *Update Key Generation by Authority*, *Secret Key Update for non-revoked Users* and *Ciphertext Update by Cloud Server*. Suppose an attribute x' is revoked from a user μ.

3.4.3.1 Update Key Generation by Authority

When there is an attribute revocation, the authority runs the update key generation algorithm **UKeyGen**$(MK, VK_{x'}) \rightarrow (\widetilde{VK}_{x'}, UK_{x'})$. It takes the master key MK and the current version key $VK_{x'}$ of the revoked attribute x' as inputs. It generates a new attribute version key $\widetilde{VK}_{x'}$ by randomly choosing a number $\tilde{v}_{x'} \in \mathbb{Z}_p(\tilde{v}_{x'} \neq v_{x'})$. Then, the authority computes the update key as

$$UK_{x'} = \left(UK_{1,x'} = \frac{\tilde{v}_{x'}}{v_{x'}}, \ UK_{2,x'} = \frac{v_{x'} - \tilde{v}_{x'}}{v_{x'}\gamma} \right).$$

It outputs a new version key $\widetilde{VK}_{x'}$ of the attribute x' and an update key $UK_{x'}$ that can be used for updating the secret keys of non-revoked users and the ciphertexts that are associated with the revoked attribute x'. Then, the authority sends the update key $UK_{x'}$ to the cloud server (for ciphertext updating) via secure channels.

The authority also updates the public attribute key of the revoked attribute x' as

$$\widetilde{PK}_{x'} = (\widetilde{PK}_{1,x'} = (PK_{1,x'})^{UK_{1,x'}}, \ \widetilde{PK}_{2,x'} = (PK_{2,x'})^{UK_{1,x'}})$$
$$= (\widetilde{PK}_{1,x'} = H(x')^{\tilde{v}_{x'}}, \ \widetilde{PK}_{2,x'} = H(x')^{\tilde{v}_{x'}\gamma}).$$

After that, the authority broadcasts a message to all the owners that the public attribute key of the revoked attribute x' is updated. Then, all the owners can obtain the new public attribute key of the revoked attribute from the public bulletin board of the authority.

3.4.3.2 Secret Key Update for Non-revoked Users

Each non-revoked user submits two components $L = g^t$ and $K_{x'}$ of the secret key SK to the authority. Upon receiving these components, the authority runs the SKUpdate to compute a new component $\tilde{K}_{x'}$ associated with the revoked attribute x' as

$$\tilde{K}_{x'} = (K_{x'}/L^{\beta^2})^{UK_{1,x'}} \cdot L^{\beta^2} = g^{t\beta^2} \cdot H(x')^{\tilde{v}_{x'}t\beta}.$$

Then, it returns the new component $\tilde{K}_{x'}$ to the non-revoked user. The user's secret key is updated by replacing the component $K_{x'}$ associated with the revoked attribute x' with the new one $\tilde{K}_{x'}$:

$$\widetilde{SK} = (\, K, \ L, \ \tilde{K}_{x'}, \ \forall x \in S \backslash \{x'\} : K_x \,).$$

Note that only the component associated with the revoked attribute x' in the secret key needs to be updated, while all the other components are kept unchanged.

3.4.3.3 Ciphertext Update by Cloud Server

To ensure that the newly joined user who has sufficient attributes can still decrypt those previous data which are published before it joined the system, all the ciphertexts associated with the revoked attribute are required to be updated to the latest version. Intuitively, the ciphertext update should be done by data owners, which will incur a heavy overhead on the data owner. To improve the efficiency, ABAC moves the workload of ciphertext update from data owners to the cloud server, such that it can eliminate the huge communication overhead between data owners and cloud server, and the heavy computation cost on data owners. The ciphertext update is conducted by using proxy re-encryption method, which means that the server does not need to decrypt the ciphertext before updating.

Upon receiving the update key UK_x from the authority. The cloud server runs the ciphertext update algorithm CTUpdate to update the ciphertext associated with the revoked attribute x'. It takes as inputs the ciphertext CT and the update key $UK_{x'}$. It updates the ciphertext associated with x' as

$$\widetilde{CT} = (\, \tilde{C} = C, \ \tilde{C}' = C', \ \forall i = 1 \ to \ l : \tilde{D}_{2,i} = D_{2,i},$$
$$if \ \rho(i) \neq x' : \ \tilde{C}_i = C_i, \ \tilde{D}_{1,i} = D_{1,i},$$
$$if \ \rho(i) = x' : \ \tilde{C}_i = C_i \cdot (D_{1,i})^{UK_{2,x'}}, \ \tilde{D}_{1,i} = (D_{1,i})^{UK_{1,x'}} \,)$$

It is obvious that ABAC only requires to update those components associated with the revoked attribute in the ciphertext, while the other components are not changed. In this way, ABAC can greatly improve the efficiency of attribute revocation.

The ciphertext update can not only guarantee the forward security of the attribute revocation, but also can reduce the storage overhead on the users (i.e., all the users need to hold only the latest secret key, rather than to keep records on all the previous secret keys). The cloud server in ABAC is required to be semi-trusted. Even when the cloud server is not semi-trusted in some circumstance, which means that the server will not update the ciphertexts correctly. The forward security cannot be guaranteed, but ABAC can still achieve the backward security (i.e., the revoked user cannot decrypt the new published ciphertexts encrypted with the new public attribute keys).

3.5 Analysis of ABAC

3.5.1 Security Analysis

We conclude the security analysis as the following Theorems:

Theorem 3.1 *When the decisional q-parallel BDHE assumption holds, no polynomial time adversary can selectively break ABAC with a challenge matrix of size* $l^* \times n^*$, *where* $n^* \leq q$.

Proof Suppose we have an adversary $\mathcal{A}$ with non-negligible advantage $\varepsilon = Adv_{\mathcal{A}}$ in the selective security game against the construction of ABAC and suppose it chooses a challenge matrix M^* with the dimension at most q columns. Under the constraint that none of the updated secret keys $\widetilde{SK}$ (generated by both the queried secret keys SKs and update keys UKs) can decrypt the challenge ciphertext, we can build a simulator $\mathcal{B}$ that plays the decisional q-parallel BDHE problem with non-negligible advantage.   □

Theorem 3.2 *ABAC is secure against the unauthorized access.*

Proof From the definition of the unauthorized access, there are two scenarios: (1) Users who do not have sufficient attributes satisfying the access structure may try to access and decrypt the data. (2) When one or some attributes of the user are revoked, the user may still try to access the data with his/her previous secret key.

For the first scenario, the users who do not have sufficient attributes cannot decrypt the ciphertext by using their own secret keys. We also consider the collusion attack from multiple users, in ABAC, the user's secret key is generated with a random number, such that they may not be the same even if the users have the same set of attributes. Thus, they cannot collude their secret keys together to decrypt the ciphertext.

For the second scenario, suppose one attribute is revoked from a user, the authority will choose another version key to generate the update key and sends it to the server for updating all the ciphertexts associated with the revoked attribute, such that the ciphertexts are associated with the latest version key of the revoked attributes. Due to the different values of the version key in the ciphertext, the revoked user is not able to use the previous secret key to decrypt the ciphertext.   □

Table 3.1 Comparison of each component size

Component	ABAC	[6]
Master key	$4\|p\|$	$\|p\| + \|g\|$
Public key	$2\|g\| + \|g_T\|$	$2\|g\| + \|g_T\|$
Secret key	$2\|g\| + n_{a,i} \cdot \|g\|$	$\|g\| + 2n_{a,i} \cdot \|g\|$
Other keys	$\|p\|^a + 2\|g\|^b$	$\log(n_u + 1) \cdot \|p\|^c$
Ciphertext	$\|g_T\| + (3l + 1)\|g\|$	$\|g_T\| + (2l + 1)\|g\| + \frac{l \cdot \|n_u\| \cdot \|p\|}{2}$

[a]Version key; [b]Update key; [c]Path Key
n_a total number of attributes in the system
n_u total number of users in the system
$n_{a,i}$ number of attributes the user i possesses
l number of attributes associated with the ciphertext

3.5.2 Performance Analysis

We give the analysis of ABAC by comparing with [6] in terms of storage overhead, communication cost and computation efficiency. Let $|p|$ be the size of elements in $\mathbb{Z}_p$. Let $|g|$ and $|g_T|$ be the element size in $\mathbb{G}$ and $\mathbb{G}_T$ respectively. First, we compare each component involved in ABAC and [6], as described in Table 3.1.

3.5.2.1 Storage Overhead

Table 3.2 shows the comparison of storage overhead on each entity in the system. The main storage overhead on the authority comes from the master key in [6]. Besides the master key, in ABAC, the authority needs to hold a version key for each attribute. Both the public parameters and the public attribute keys contribute the storage overhead on the owner in ABAC, which is linear to the total number of attributes in the system. Although the data is stored on the server in the format as shown in Fig. 3.2, we do not consider the storage overhead caused by the encrypted data, which are the same in both ABAC and [6]. ABAC only requires the server to store the ciphertext, while the server in [6] needs to store both the message head and the ciphertext which is also linear to the number of users in the system. The storage overhead on each user in

Table 3.2 Comparison of storage overhead

Entity	ABAC	[6]
Authority	$(4 + n_a) \cdot \|p\|$	$2\|p\|$
Owner	$(2 + n_a)\|g\| + \|g_T\|$	$2\|g\| + \|g_T\|$
Server	$\|g_T\| + (3l + 1)\|g\|$	$2\|g_T\| + (3l + 3)\|g\| + \frac{l \cdot \|n_u\| \cdot \|p\|}{2}$
User	$(2 + n_{a,i}) \cdot \|g\|$	$(2n_{a,i} + 1)\|g\| + \log(n_u + 1)\|p\|$

n_a total number of attributes in the system
n_u total number of users in the system
$n_{a,i}$ number of attributes the user i possesses
l number of attributes associated with the ciphertext

ABAC is associated with the number of attributes it possesses, while in [6] the storage overhead on each user is not only linear to the number of attributes it possesses but also linear to the number of users in the system. Usually, the number of users are much larger than the number of attributes in the system, which means that ABAC incurs less storage overhead.

3.5.2.2 Communication Cost

As illustrated in Table 3.3, the communication cost in the system is mainly caused by the keys and ciphertexts. In ABAC, the communication cost between the authority and the user comes from both the user's secret keys and the update keys, while in [6] only the secret key contributes the communication cost between the authority and the user. The communication cost between the authority and the owner mainly comes from the public keys. In ABAC, when there is an attribute revocation, the owner needs to get the latest public attribute key of the revoked attributes, which also contributes the communication between the authority and the owner.

In ABAC, the communication cost between the server and the user comes from the ciphertext. But in [6], besides the ciphertext, the message head (which contains the path keys) also contributes the communication cost between the server and the users, which is linear with the number of all the users in the system. Thus, ABAC incurs less communication cost between the server and the user than [6]. The ciphertext contributes the main communication cost between the server and the owner. Because the size of ciphertext in ABAC is much smaller than the one in [6], the communication cost between the sever and the owner is much less than the one in [6].

3.5.2.3 Computation Efficiency

The implementations of ABAC and [6] are conducted on a Linux system with an Intel Core 2 Duo CPU at 3.16 GHz and 4.00 GB RAM. The code uses the Pairing-Based Cryptography (PBC) library version 0.5.12 to implement the schemes. A symmetric elliptic curve α-curve is used during the simulation, where the base field size is 512-bit and the embedding degree is 2. The α-curve has a 160-bit group order, which

Table 3.3 Comparison of communication cost

Communication Cost between	ABAC	[6]
Auth.&User	$4\lvert g\rvert + n_{a,i}\lvert g\rvert$	$\lvert g\rvert + 2n_{a,i}\lvert g\rvert$
Auth.&Owner	$2\lvert g\rvert + \lvert g_T\rvert + n_a\lvert g\rvert$	$2\lvert g\rvert + \lvert g_T\rvert$
Server&User	$\lvert g_T\rvert + (3l+1)\lvert g\rvert$	$\lvert g_T\rvert + (2l+1)\lvert g\rvert +$ $(l \cdot \lvert n_u\rvert/2 + \log(n_u + 1))\lvert p\rvert$
Server&Owner	$\lvert G_T\rvert + (3l+1) \cdot \lvert G\rvert$	$(l+1)\lvert G_T\rvert + 2l\lvert G\rvert$

n_a total number of attributes in the system
n_u total number of users in the system
$n_{a,i}$ number of attributes the user i possesses
l number of attributes associated with the ciphertext

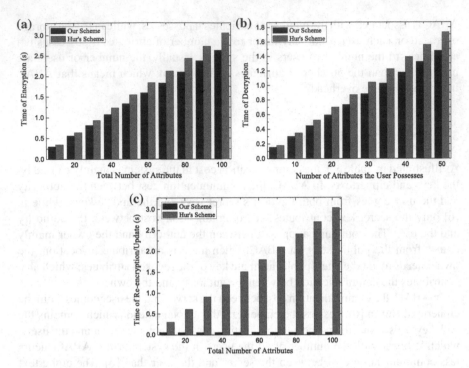

Fig. 3.3 Computation cost comparison. **a** Encryption, **b** Decryption, **c** Re-encryption

means p is a 160-bit length prime. The size of the plaintext is set to be 1 KByte. All the simulation results are the mean of 20 trials.

We compare the computation efficiency between ABAC and [6] in terms of encryption, decryption and re-encryption.[3] From the Fig. 3.3a, we can see that the time of encryption is linear with the total number of attributes in the system. The encryption phase in ABAC is more efficient than the one in [6]. That is because, in [6], the owner first encrypts the data by using the CP-ABE scheme and sends the ciphertext to the server. Upon receiving the ciphertext from the owner, the server will re-encrypt the ciphertext with a randomly generated encryption exponent. Then, the server encrypts this exponent with a set of attribute group keys by using the broadcast encryption approach. Correspondingly, in the phase of decryption, the user should first decrypt the exponent with its own path key and uses it to decrypt the data together with the secret key. In ABAC, however, the user only needs to use the secret key to decrypt the data, which is more efficient than the [6] as illustrated in the Fig. 3.3b.

During the attribute revocation, ABAC only requires to update those components associated with the revoked attribute of the ciphertext, while the [6] should re-encrypt all the components of the ciphertext. Besides, the re-encryption in [6] should generate

---

[3] Note that we do not consider the computation of symmetric encryption for data components since they are the same in both ABAC and [6].

a new encryption exponent and encrypt this new exponent with the new set of attribute group key by using broadcast encryption approach. Thus, as illustrated in Fig. 3.3c, the time of re-encryption phase in [6] is linear with the total number of attributes, while the time of ciphertext update in ABAC is constant to the number of revoked attributes.

3.6 Related Work

The traditional remote storage systems usually rely on the cryptographic techniques to conduct data access control. In [8], data owners encrypt files by using the symmetric encryption approach with content keys and then use every user's public key to encrypt the content keys. The key management in this approach is very complicated when there are a large number of data owners and users. Also, the key distribution is not convenient in the situation of user dynamically joining or leaving the system, since it requires each data owner to always be online. To deal with the key distribution issue, Goh et al. [4] proposed a SiRiUS to provide the end-to-end security over the existing file systems, such as NFS. It attaches each file with a metadata file that contains the file's access control list (ACL), each entry of which is the encryption of the content key by using the public key of each user. The extension version of SiRiUS applied NNL broadcast encryption algorithm [12] to encrypt the content key instead of encrypting it with each individual user's public key. However, these access control techniques cannot be applied in cloud storage systems, because the data owner does not know which potential user can access its data before the encryption.

Some methods are proposed by delivering the key management and distribution from data owners to the remote server under the assumption that the server is trusted or semi-trusted [3, 18–20]. In [3], the authors divide users into groups based on their access rights to the data. To reduce the number of encryption keys, the users are then organized into a hierarchy and further transformed to a tree structure. In [20], the data owner's data is encrypted block-by-block and a binary key tree is constructed over the block keys to reduce the number of keys given to each user. In [19], Vimercati et al. proposed a fine-grained access control for the outsourced data on semi-trusted servers. It allows the server to conduct a second level encryption (over-encryption) to control access, while the complexities of file encryption and user grant/revocation operations are linear to the number of authorized users. They also proposed another access control scheme which required the server to store multiple copies of the same data encrypted by different keys [18]. But it may cause heavy storage overhead and the server should be fully trusted. These schemes, however, are inappropriate to the problem because the server is not trustworthy in cloud storage systems.

The attribute-based encryption (ABE) technique [2, 5, 15, 21] is regarded as one of the most suitable technologies for data access control in cloud storage systems, because it allows the data owner to define the access policy on the attributes instead of on the users. There are two complementary forms of ABE, Key-Policy ABE (KP-ABE) [5] and Ciphertext-Policy ABE (CP-ABE) [2, 21]. In KP-ABE, attributes are used to describe the encrypted data and access policies over these attributes are built into user's secret keys; while in CP-ABE, attributes are used to describe the user's attributes and the access policies over these attributes are attached to the encrypted data.

In [23], the authors proposed a fine-grained data access control scheme based on the KP-ABE approach [5]. In their scheme, the data owner encrypts the data with a content key and then encrypt the content key by using the KP-ABE technique. The data owner assigns the access structure and the corresponding secret key to users by encrypting them with the user's public key and stores it on the server. However, their scheme requires the data owner to always be online for user joining, which is not appropriate in cloud storage systems. Some access control schemes are proposed based on CP-ABE [2, 6], since CP-ABE is considered to be more suitable for data access control in cloud storage systems than KP-ABE. It allows data owners to define an access structure on attributes and encrypt the data under this access structure, such that data owners can define the attributes that the user needs to possess in order to decrypt the ciphertext. In [10], the author proposed a proxy re-encryption method for ABE systems that allows the proxy to transform the access policy of the ciphertext into another one. However, the revocation issue in CP-ABE is still an open problem.

To deal with the attribute revocation issue in ABE system, Pirretti et al. [14] proposed a timed rekeying mechanism, which is implemented by setting expiration time on each attribute. However, this approach requires the users to periodically go to the authority for key update. This brings a heavy burden to the authority and thus is inefficient. In [2], the authors improve the Pirretti's scheme by assigning the user's secret key with a single expiration date instead of on each attribute, such that the keys could be updated less frequently. In [9], the authors proposed a multi-authority ciphertext-policy ABE scheme with accountability. In [22], the authors also improved the efficiency and proposed a temporal attribute revocation based on the timed rekeying methods for cloud storage systems with multiple authorities. However, these schemes can just disable a user's secret key at a designated time, while the immediate attribute revocation cannot be realized.

Golle et al. [17] proposed a user revocable KP-ABE scheme, with the condition that the number of attributes associated with a ciphertext is exactly half of the universe size. Some previous revocation schemes [11, 13] only allow the user level revocation. That is when a user is revoked even from a single attribute group, it loses all the access rights to the data in the system. In [1], the authors proposed a user-revocable ABE systems by combining broadcast encryption schemes with ABE schemes. This scheme, however, requires the data owner to maintain all the membership list for each attribute group, which is not applicable in cloud storage systems.

Yu et al. [24] proposed an attribute revocation method for CP-ABE, where the authority redefines the master key components for involved attributes and generates the new public keys for re-encrypting the ciphertext and new secret keys for users. But they delegate the re-encryption of ciphertext and the secret key update to the server. However, like the method in [7], but they require the server to decide which users can update their secret keys according to the revoked user identity list, such that the server is required to be fully trusted.

Hur et al. [6] also proposed an attribute revocation scheme in CP-ABE by allowing the server to re-encrypt the ciphertext with a set of attribute group keys. It can conduct the access right revocation on attribute level rather than on user level. During the attribute revocation, the server needs to change the attribute group key for the attribute which is affected by the membership change and re-encrypts the ciphertext with the new set of group attribute keys. This may incur high computation cost on the server. Also the server should be fully trusted. However, the server in cloud storage systems cannot be trusted and thus [6] cannot be applied in the problem. Therefore, the attribute revocation is still an open problem in attribute-based data access control.

3.7 Conclusion

In this chapter, we described an attribute-based fine-grained data access control scheme, ABAC, where the owner was in charge of defining and enforcing the access policy. We also presented an efficient attribute revocation method for CP-ABE, which can greatly reduce the cost of attribute revocation.

References

1. Attrapadung, N., Imai, H.: Conjunctive broadcast and attribute-based encryption. In: Proceedings of the Third International Conference on Pairing-Based Cryptography (Pairing'09), pp. 248–265. Springer (2009)
2. Bethencourt, J., Sahai, A., Waters, B.: Ciphertext-policy attribute-based encryption. In: Proceedings of the 2007 IEEE Symposium on Security and Privacy (S&P'07), pp. 321–334. IEEE Computer Society (2007)
3. Damiani, E., di Vimercati, S.D.C., Foresti, S., Jajodia, S., Paraboschi, S., Samarati, P.: Key management for multi-user encrypted databases. In: Proceedings of the 2005 ACM Workshop On Storage Security And Survivability (StorageSS'05), pp. 74–83. ACM (2005)
4. Goh, E.J., Shacham, H., Modadugu, N., Boneh, D.: Sirius: securing remote untrusted storage. In: Proceedings of the Network and Distributed System Security Symposium (NDSS'03). The Internet Society (2003)
5. Goyal, V., Pandey, O., Sahai, A., Waters, B.: Attribute-based encryption for fine-grained access control of encrypted data. In: Proceedings of the 13th ACM Conference on Computer and Communications Security (CCS'06), pp. 89–98. ACM (2006)
6. Hur, J., Noh, D.K.: Attribute-based access control with efficient revocation in data outsourcing systems. IEEE Trans. Parallel Distrib. Syst. 22(7), 1214–1221 (2011)
7. Jahid, S., Mittal, P., Borisov, N.: Easier: encryption-based access control in social networks with efficient revocation. In: Proceedings of the 6th ACM Symposium on Information, Computer and Communications Security (ASIACCS'11), pp. 411–415. ACM (2011)
8. Kallahalla, M., Riedel, E., Swaminathan, R., Wang, Q., Fu, K.: Plutus: scalable secure file sharing on untrusted storage. In: Proceedings of the 2nd USENIX Conference on File and Storage Technologies (FAST'03). USENIX (2003)
9. Li, J., Huang, Q., Chen, X., Chow, S.S.M., Wong, D.S., Xie, D.: Multi-authority ciphertext-policy attribute-based encryption with accountability. In: Proceedings of the 6th ACM Symposium on Information, Computer and Communications Security (ASIACCS'11), pp. 386–390. ACM (2011)

10. Liang, X., Cao, Z., Lin, H., Shao, J.: Attribute based proxy re-encryption with delegating capabilities. In: Proceedings of the 2009 ACM Symposium on Information, Computer and Communications Security, ASIACCS'09, pp. 276–286. ACM (2009)

11. Liang, X., Lu, R., Lin, X.: Ciphertext policy attribute based encryption with efficient revocation. University of Waterloo, Technical Report (2011)

12. Naor, D., Naor, M., Lotspiech, J.: Revocation and tracing schemes for stateless receivers. In: Electronic Colloquium on Computational Complexity (ECCC) (2002)

13. Ostrovsky, R., Sahai, A., Waters, B.: Attribute-based encryption with non-monotonic access structures. In: Proceedings of the 14th ACM Conference on Computer and Communications Security (CCS'07), pp. 195–203. ACM (2007)

14. Pirretti, M., Traynor, P., McDaniel, P., Waters, B.: Secure attribute-based systems. In: Proceedings of the 13th ACM Conference on Computer and Communications Security (CCS'06), pp. 99–112. ACM (2006)

15. Sahai, A., Waters, B.: Fuzzy identity-based encryption. In: Proceedings of the 24th Annual International Conference on the Theory and Applications of Cryptographic Techniques: Advances in Cryptology—EUROCRYPT'05, pp. 457–473. Springer (2005)

16. Sohr, K., Drouineaud, M., Ahn, G.J., Gogolla, M.: Analyzing and managing role-based access control policies. IEEE Trans. Knowl. Data Eng. **20**(7), 924–939 (2008)

17. Staddon, J., Golle, P., Gagné, M., Rasmussen, P.: A content-driven access control system. In: Proceedings of the 7th Symposium on Identity and Trust on the Internet (IDtrust'08), pp. 26–35. ACM (2008)

18. di Vimercati, S.D.C., Foresti, S., Jajodia, S., Paraboschi, S., Samarati, P.: A data outsourcing architecture combining cryptography and access control. In: Proceedings of the 2007 ACM workshop on Computer Security Architecture (CSAW'07), pp. 63–69. ACM (2007)

19. di Vimercati, S.D.C., Foresti, S., Jajodia, S., Paraboschi, S., Samarati, P.: Over-encryption: management of access control evolution on outsourced data. In: Proceedings of the 33rd International Conference on Very Large Data Bases (VLDB'07), pp. 123–134. ACM (2007)

20. Wang, W., Li, Z., Owens, R., Bhargava, B.K.: Secure and efficient access to outsourced data. In: Proceedings of the First ACM Cloud Computing Security Workshop (CCSW'09), pp. 55–66. ACM (2009)

21. Waters, B.: Ciphertext-policy attribute-based encryption: An expressive, efficient, and provably secure realization. In: Proceedings of the 4th International Conference on Practice and Theory in Public Key Cryptography (PKC'11), pp. 53–70. Springer (2011)

22. Yang, K., Liu, Z., et al.: TAAC: temporal attribute-based access control for multi-authority cloud storage systems. IACR Cryptology ePrint Archive, p. 772 (2012)

23. Yu, S., Wang, C., Ren, K., Lou, W.: Achieving secure, scalable, and fine-grained data access control in cloud computing. In: Proceedings of the 29th IEEE International Conference on Computer Communications (INFOCOM'10), pp. 534–542. IEEE (2010)

24. Yu, S., Wang, C., Ren, K., Lou, W.: Attribute based data sharing with attribute revocation. In: Proceedings of the 5th ACM Symposium on Information, Computer and Communications Security (ASIACCS'10), pp. 261–270. ACM (2010)

Chapter 4
DAC-MACS: Effective Data Access Control for Multi-Authority Cloud Storage Systems

Abstract Ciphertext-Policy Attribute-based Encryption (CP-ABE) is a promising technique for access control of encrypted data, which requires a trusted authority to manage all the attributes and distributes keys in the system. In multi-authority cloud storage systems, the users' attributes come from different domains each of which is managed by a different authority. However, existing CP-ABE schemes cannot be directly applied to data access control for multi-authority cloud storage systems, due to the inefficiency of decryption and revocation. In this chapter, we propose DAC-MACS (Data Access Control for Multi-Authority Cloud Storage), an effective and secure data access control scheme with efficient decryption and revocation.

4.1 Introduction

Ciphertext-Policy Attribute-based Encryption (CP-ABE) [2, 25] is regarded as one of the most suitable technologies for data access control in cloud storage systems, because it gives the data owner more direct control on access policies and does not require the data owner to distribute keys. In CP-ABE scheme, there is an authority that is responsible for attribute management and key distribution. The authority can be the registration office in a university, the human resource department in a company, etc. The data owner defines the access policies and encrypts data under the policies. Each user will be issued a secret key reflecting its attributes. A user can decrypt the ciphertexts only when its attributes satisfy the access policies.

Extensive research has been done for single authority systems [2, 8, 14, 21, 25]. However, in cloud storage systems, a user may hold attributes issued by multiple authorities and the owner may share data with the users administrated to different authorities. For instance, in an E-healthy system, the medical data may be shared only with a user who has the attribute of "Doctor" issued by a hospital and the attribute "Medical Researcher" issued by a medical research center. Although some multi-authority CP-ABE schemes [3, 4, 15, 19] have been proposed for data encryption,

K. Yang and X. Jia, *Security for Cloud Storage Systems*, SpringerBriefs
in Computer Science, DOI: 10.1007/978-1-4614-7873-7_4,
© The Author(s) 2014

they cannot be directly applied to data access control for multi-authority cloud storage systems, because they either require a global central attribute authority to manage all the attributes across different organizations or lack of efficiency. In this chapter, we investigate the data access control issue in multi-authority cloud storage systems.

One critical requirement in the design of access control schemes is the *efficiency in computation*. There are two operations in access control that require efficient computation, namely *decryption* and *revocation*. The users may use their smart phones to access the data in nowadays cloud storage systems, but the computation ability of smart phones is not as strong as the PCs. Thus, the decryption on each user should be as efficient as possible in data access control schemes. When a user is degraded or leaving the system, some attributes should be revoked from this user. There are two requirements of the efficient attribute revocation: (1) The revoked user (whose attribute is revoked) cannot decrypt the new ciphertexts that require the revoked attributes to decrypt (Backward Security); (2) The newly joined user can also decrypt the previously published ciphertexts that are encrypted with previous public keys if it has sufficient attributes (Forward Security).

In this chapter, we first introduce DAC-MACS (Data Access Control for Multi-Authority Cloud Storage), an effective and secure data access control scheme with efficient decryption and revocation for multi-authority cloud storage systems, which is provably secure in the random oracle model and has better performance than existing schemes. The efficient immediate attribute revocation method in DAC-MACS achieves both forward security and backward security.

4.2 System Model and Security Model

4.2.1 System Model

As shown in Fig. 4.1, DAC-MACS consists of five types of entities: a global certificate authority (CA), the attribute authorities (*AA*s), the cloud server (server), the data owners (owners) and the data consumers (users).

The CA is a global trusted certificate authority in the system. It sets up the system and accepts the registration of all the users and *AA*s in the system. For each legal user in the system, the CA assigns a global unique user identity to it and also generates a pair of global secret key and global public key for this user. However, the CA is *not* involved in any attribute management and any generation of secret keys that are associated with attributes. For example, the CA can be the Social Security Administration, an independent agency of the United States government. Each user will be issued a Social Security Number (SSN) as its global identity.

Every *AA* is an independent attribute authority that is responsible for entitling, revoking and updating user's attributes according to their role or identity in its domain. In DAC-MACS, every attribute is associated with a single *AA*, but each *AA* can manage an arbitrary number of attributes. Every *AA* has full control over the structure

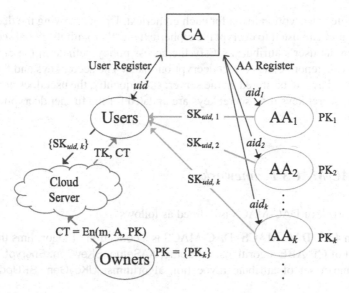

Fig. 4.1 System model of DAC-MACS

and semantics of its attributes. Each *AA* is responsible for generating a public attribute key for each attribute it manages and a secret key for each user reflecting their attributes.

The cloud server stores the owners' data and provides data access service to users. It helps the user decrypt a ciphertext by generating a decryption token of the ciphertext according to user's secret keys issued by the *AA*s. The server also does the ciphertext update when an attribute revocation happens.

Each owner first divides the data into several components according to the logic granularities and encrypts each data component with different content keys by using symmetric encryption techniques. Then, the owner defines the access policies over attributes from multiple attribute authorities and encrypts the content keys under the policies. Then, the owner sends the encrypted data to the cloud server together with the ciphertexts.[1] They do not rely on the server to do data access control. Instead, the ciphertext can be accessed by all the legal users in the system, which means that any legal user who has been authenticated by the system somehow, he/she can freely query any interested ciphertexts from the server. But, the *access control happens inside the cryptography*. That is only when the user's attributes satisfy the access policy defined in the ciphertext, the user is able to decrypt the ciphertext. Thus, users with different attributes can decrypt different number of content keys and thus obtain different granularities of information from the same data.

Each user is assigned with a global user identity from the CA and can freely get the ciphertexts from the server. To decrypt a ciphertext, each user may submit their secret keys issued by some *AA*s together with its global public key to the server and ask

---

[1] In this chapter, we simply use the ciphertext to denote the encrypted content keys with CP-ABE.

it to generate a decryption token for each ciphertext. Upon receiving the decryption token, the user can use it to decrypt the ciphertext together with its global secret key. Only when the user's attributes satisfy the access policy defined in the ciphertext, the server can generate the correct decryption token. The secret keys and the global user's public key can be stored on the server; subsequently, the user does not need to submit any secret keys if no secret keys are updated for the further decryption token generation.

4.2.2 DAC-MACS Framework

The framework of DAC-MACS is defined as follows.

Definition 4.1 (DAC-MACS) DAC-MACS is a collection of algorithms that combines a set of CP-ABE algorithms: CASetup, AASetup, SKeyGen, Encrypt, TKGen, Decrypt and a set of attribute revocation algorithms: UKeyGen, SKUpdate and CTUpdate.

- **CASetup**$(1^\lambda) \rightarrow$ (MSK, SP, sk_{CA}, vk_{CA}, $\{(uid, \text{GPK}_{uid}, \text{GSK}_{uid}, Cert(uid))\})$. The CA setup algorithm is run by the CA. It takes no input other than the implicit security parameter λ. It outputs the master key MSK, the system parameter SP, a secret and verificative key pair (sk_{CA}, vk_{CA}) of CA. For each user uid, it generates a global public/secret key pair $(\text{GPK}_{uid}, \text{GSK}_{uid})$ and a certificate $Cert(uid)$.
- **AASetup**$(aid) \rightarrow$ $(\text{SK}_{aid}, \text{PK}_{aid}, \{\text{VK}_{x_{aid}}, \text{PK}_{x_{aid}}\})$. The attribute authority setup algorithm is run by each AA. It takes the authority identity aid as input. It outputs a pair of authority secret key SK_{aid} and authority public key PK_{aid}, the set of version keys and public attribute keys $\{\text{VK}_{x_{aid}}, \text{PK}_{x_{aid}}\}$ for all attributes x issued by the AA_{aid}.
- **SKeyGen**$(S_{uid,aid}, \text{SK}_{aid}, \{\text{PK}_{x_{aid}}\}, \text{SP}, Cert(uid)) \rightarrow \text{SK}_{uid,aid}$. The secret key generation algorithm is run by each AA. It takes as inputs a set of attributes $S_{uid,aid}$ that describes the secret key, the authority secret key SK_{aid}, the set of public attribute keys $\{\text{PK}_{x_{aid}}\}$, the system parameter SP and the certificate of the user with uid. It outputs a secret key $\text{SK}_{uid,aid}$ for the user with uid.
- **Encrypt**$(\text{SP}, \{\text{PK}_k\}_{k \in I_A}, \{\text{PK}_{x_k}\}_{x_k \in S_{A_k}}^{k \in I_A}, m, \mathbb{A}) \rightarrow CT$. The encryption algorithm is run by data owners. It takes as inputs the system parameter SP, a set of public keys $\{\text{PK}_k\}_{k \in I_A}$ from the involved authority set I_A, a set of public attribute keys $\{\text{PK}_{x_k}\}_{x_k \in S_{A_k}}^{k \in I_A}$, a message m and an access structure $\mathbb{A}$ over all the selected attributes from the involved AAs. The algorithm encrypts m according to the access structure $\mathbb{A}$ and outputs a ciphertext CT. It is assumed that the ciphertext implicitly contains the access structure $\mathbb{A}$.
- **TKGen**$(CT, \text{GPK}_{uid}, \{\text{SK}_{uid,k}\}_{k \in I_A}) \rightarrow \text{TK}$. The decryption token generation algorithm is run by the cloud server. It takes as inputs the ciphertext CT which contains an access structure $\mathbb{A}$, user's global public key GPK_{uid} and a set of user's secret keys

$\{SK_{uid,k}\}_{k \in I_A}$. If the set of attributes S satisfies the access structure $\mathbb{A}$, the algorithm can successfully compute the correct decryption token TK of the ciphertext.

- **Decrypt**(CT, TK, GSK_{uid}) → m. The decryption algorithm is run by the users. It takes as inputs the ciphertext CT, the decryption token TK and the user's global secret key GSK_{uid}. It outputs the message m.
- **UKeyGen**(SK_{aid}, $\{u_j\}$, $VK_{\tilde{x}_{aid}}$) → ($KUK_{j,\tilde{x}_{aid}}$, $CUK_{\tilde{x}_{aid}}$). The update key generation algorithm is run by the AA corresponding to the revoked attribute $\tilde{x}_{aid}$. It takes as inputs the authority secret key SK_{aid}, a set of user's secret $\{u_j\}$ and the previous version key of the revoked attribute $VK_{\tilde{x}_{aid}}$. It outputs both the user's Key Update Key $KUK_{j,\tilde{x}_{aid}}$ ($j \in S_U, j \neq \mu, \tilde{x}_{aid} \in S_{j,aid}$) and the Ciphertext Update Key $CUK_{\tilde{x}_{aid}}$.
- **SKUpdate**($SK_{uid,aid}$, $KUK_{uid,\tilde{x}_{aid}}$) → $SK'_{uid,aid}$. The user's secret key update algorithm is run by all the non-revoked users. It takes as inputs the current secret key $SK_{uid,aid}$ and its key update key $KUK_{uid,\tilde{x}_{aid}}$. It outputs a new secret key $SK'_{uid,aid}$.
- **CTUpdate**(CT, $CUK_{\tilde{x}_{aid}}$) → CT'. The ciphertext update algorithm is run by the cloud server. It takes as inputs the current ciphertext CT and the ciphertext update key $CUK_{\tilde{x}_{aid}}$. It outputs a new ciphertext CT'.

4.2.3 Security Model

4.2.3.1 Threat Model

In multi-authority cloud storage systems, the CA is assumed to be trusted in the system. But we still need to prevent it from decrypting any ciphertexts. Each AA is also assumed to be trusted, and can be corrupted by the adversary. The server is assumed to be curious but honest. It is curious about the content of the encrypted data or the received message, but will execute correctly the task assigned by each AA. The users are assumed to be dishonest and may collude to obtain unauthorized access to data. DAC-MACS also assumes that all the non-revoked users will not give the received update keys to the revoked user.

4.2.3.2 Decisional q-Parallel Bilinear Diffie-Hellman Exponent Assumption

We recall the definition of the decisional q-parallel Bilinear Diffie-Hellman Exponent (q-parallel BDHE) problem in [25] as follows. Chooses a group $\mathbb{G}$ of prime order p according to the security parameter. Let $a, s \in \mathbb{Z}_p$ be chosen at random and g be a generator of $\mathbb{G}$. If an adversary is given

$$\mathbf{y} = (\, g, g^s, g^{1/z}, g^{a/z}, \ldots, g^{(a^q/z)},$$

$$g^a, \ldots, g^{(a^q)}, g^{(a^{q+2})}, \ldots, g^{(a^{2q})},$$

$$\forall_{1 \le j \le q} \; g^{s \cdot b_j}, g^{a/b_j}, \ldots, g^{(a^q/b_j)}, g^{(a^{q+2}/b_j)}, \ldots, g^{(a^{2q}/b_j)},$$

$$\forall_{1 \le j, k \le q, k \neq j} \; g^{a \cdot s \cdot b_k/b_j}, \ldots, g^{(a^q \cdot s \cdot b_k/b_j)} \,),$$

it must be hard to distinguish a valid tuple $e(g, g)^{a^{q+1}s} \in \mathbb{G}_T$ from a random element R in $\mathbb{G}_T$.

An algorithm $\mathcal{B}$ that outputs $z \in \{0, 1\}$ has advantage ε in solving q-parallel BDHE in $\mathbb{G}$ if

$$\left| Pr[\mathcal{B}(\mathbf{y}, T = e(g, g)^{a^{q+1}s}) = 0] - Pr[\mathcal{B}(\mathbf{y}, T = R) = 0] \right| \ge \varepsilon.$$

Definition 4.2 The decisional q-parallel BDHE assumption holds if no polynomial time algorithm has a non-negligible advantage in solving the q-parallel BDHE problem.

4.2.3.3 Security Model

We now describe the security model of DAC-MACS by the following game between a challenger and an adversary. The security model allows the adversary to query for any secret keys and update keys that cannot be used to decrypt the challenge ciphertext. Similar to [15], the adversaries are assumed to be able to corrupt authorities only statically, but key queries are made adaptively. Let S_A denote the set of all the authorities. The security game is defined as follows.

- **Setup**. The system parameters are generated by running the CA setup algorithm. The adversary specifies a set of corrupted attribute authorities $S'_A \subset S_A$. The challenger generates the public keys by querying the AA setup oracle, and generates the secret keys by querying the secret key generation oracle. For uncorrupted authorities in $S_A - S'_A$, the challenger sends only the public keys to the adversary. For corrupted authorities in S'_A, the challenger sends both public keys and secret keys to the adversary.
- **Phase 1**. The adversary makes secret key queries by submitting pairs (uid, S_{uid}) to the challenger, where $S_{uid} = \{S_{uid,k}\}_{k \in S_A - S'_A}$ is a set of attributes belonging to several uncorrupted AAs. The challenger gives the corresponding secret keys $\{SK_{uid,k}\}$ to the adversary. The adversary also makes update key queries by submitting a set of attributes S'_{aid}. The challenger responses the corresponding update keys to the adversary.
- **Challenge**. The adversary submits two equal length messages m_0 and m_1. In addition, the adversary gives a challenge access structure (M^*, ρ^*) which must satisfy the following constraints. Let V denote the subset of rows of M^* labeled by attributes controlled by corrupted AAs. For each uid, let V_{uid} denote the subset

of rows of M^* labeled by attributes that the adversary has queried. For each uid, DAC-MACS requires that the subspace spanned by $V \cup V_{uid}$ must not include $(1, 0, \ldots, 0)$. In other words, the adversary cannot ask for a set of keys that allow decryption, in combination with any keys that can obtained from corrupted AAs. The challenger then flips a random coin b, and encrypts m_b under the access structure (M^*, ρ^*). Then, the ciphertext CT^* is given to the adversary.

- **Phase 2**. The adversary may query more secret keys and update keys, as long as they do not violate the constraints on the challenge access structure (M^*, ρ^*) and the following constraints: None of the updated secret keys (generated by the queried update keys and the queried secret keys[2]) are able to decrypt the challenged ciphertexts. In other words, the adversary is not able to query the update keys that can update the queried secret keys to the new secret keys that can decrypt the challenge ciphertext.
- **Guess**. The adversary outputs a guess b' of b.

The advantage of an adversary $\mathcal{A}$ in this game is defined as $Pr[b' = b] - \frac{1}{2}$.

Definition 4.3 DAC-MACS is secure against static corruption of authorities if all polynomial time adversaries have at most a negligible advantage in the above security game.

4.3 DAC-MACS: Data Access Control for Multi-Authority Cloud Storage

In this section, we first give an overview of the challenges and techniques of designing access control schemes for multi-authority cloud storage systems. Then, we propose the detailed construction of DAC-MACS with efficient decryption and revocation.

4.3.1 Overview

Although the existing multi-authority CP-ABE scheme [15] proposed by Lewko and Waters has high policy expressiveness and has been extended to support attribute revocation in [10], it still cannot be applied to access control for multi-authority cloud storage systems due to the inefficiency of decryption and revocation. Thus, the main challenge is to design a new underlying multi-authority CP-ABE scheme with efficient decryption and revocation.

One challenging issue in the design of a multi-authority CP-ABE scheme is how to tie the secret keys together and prevent the collusion attack. Similar to [3],

---

[2] There is another reason that makes the queried secret keys cannot decrypt the challenge ciphertext. That is at least one of the attributes in the previous queried secret keys may be not in the current version.

DAC-MACS separates the authority into a global certificate authority (CA) and multiple attribute authorities (AAs). The CA sets up the system and assigns a global user identity *uid* to each user and a global authority identity *aid* to each attribute authority in the system. Since the *uid* is globally unique in the system, secret keys issued by different AAs for the same *uid* can be tied together for decryption. Also, since each AA is associated with an *aid*, every attribute is distinguishable even though some AAs may issue the same attribute. Thus, the collusion attack can be resisted by using the *aid* and *uid*. However, different from [3], the CA in DAC-MACS is *not* involved in any attribute management and the creation of secret keys reflecting the user's attributes. DAC-MACS also requires all the AAs to generate their own public keys and uses them to encrypt data together with the global public parameters, instead of using the system unique public key (generated by the unique master key) to encrypt data. This solves the security drawback in [3], i.e., it prevents the CA from decrypting the ciphertexts.

To achieve efficient decryption on the user, DAC-MACS proposes a token-based decryption outsourcing method. It applies the decryption outsourcing idea from [10] and extends it to multiple authority systems by letting the CA generate a global secret/public key pair for each legal user in the system. During the decryption, the user submits its secret keys issued by AAs to the server and asks the server to compute a decryption token for the ciphertext. The user can decrypt the ciphertext by using the decryption token together with its global secret key.

To solve the attribute revocation problem, DAC-MACS assigns a version number for each attribute, such that when an attribute revocation happens, only those components associated with the revoked attribute in secret keys and ciphertexts need to be updated. When an attribute of a user is revoked from any AA, the AA generates a new version key for this revoked attribute and generates the update keys which contains a ciphertext update key and a set of user's key update keys. With the user's key update key, each non-revoked user who holds the revoked attributes can update its secret key. Because the update keys are associated with the *uid*, the revoked user cannot update its secret key by using other users' update keys (Backward Security). By using the ciphertext update key, the components associated with the revoked in the ciphertext can be updated to the current version. To improve the efficiency, DAC-MACS delegates the workload of ciphertext update to the server by using the proxy re-encryption method, such that the newly joined user is also able to decrypt the previous data which are published before it joins the system (Forward Security). Moreover, all the users need to hold only the latest secret key, rather than to keep records on all the previous secret keys.

4.3.2 Construction of DAC-MACS

Let S_A and S_U denote the set of attribute authorities and the set of users in the system respectively. Let $\mathbb{G}$ and $\mathbb{G}_T$ be the multiplicative groups with the same prime order p and $e : \mathbb{G} \times \mathbb{G} \rightarrow \mathbb{G}_T$ be the bilinear map. Let g be the generator of $\mathbb{G}$. Let $H : \{0, 1\}^* \rightarrow \mathbb{G}$ be a hash function such that the security is in the random oracle.

The DAC-MACS consists of five phases: System Initialization, Secret Key Generation by *AAs*, Dat Encryption by Owners, Data Decryption by Users (with the help of Cloud Server) and Attribute Revocation. For clarity, the attribute revocation phase will be described in the next section.

4.3.2.1 System Initialization

There are two steps in the system initialization phase: CA Setup and *AA* Setup.

1. *CA Setup*

   The CA runs the CA setup algorithm CASetup, which takes a security parameter as input. The CA first chooses a random number $a \in \mathbb{Z}_p$ as the master key MSK of the system and compute the system parameter $\mathsf{SP} = g^a$. Then, the CA generates a pair of secret key and verificative key (sk_{CA}, vk_{CA}). The CA accepts both *User Registration* and *AA Registration*.

   - *User Registration*

     Every user should register itself to the CA during the system initialization. If the user is legal in the system, the CA then assigns a global unique user identity *uid* to this user. For each user with *uid*, it generates the global public key $\mathsf{GPK}_{uid} = g^{u_{uid}}$ and the global secret key $\mathsf{GSK}_{uid} = z_{uid}$ by randomly choosing two numbers $u_{uid}, z_{uid} \in \mathbb{Z}_p$. The CA also generates a certificate $Cert(uid)$ which contains an item $En_{sk_{CA}}(uid, u_{uid}, g^{1/z_{uid}})$. Then, the CA gives the global public key GPK_{uid}, the global secret key GSK_{uid} and the user's certificate $Cert(uid)$ to this user.

   - *AA Registration*

     Each *AA* should also register itself to the CA during the system initialization. If the *AA* is a legal authority in the system, the CA first assigns a global authority identity *aid* to this *AA*. Then, the CA sends both its verificative key vk_{CA} and the system parameter SP to this *AA*.

2. *AA Setup*

   Each $AA_k (k \in S_A)$ runs the *AA* setup algorithm AASetup. Let S_{A_k} denote the set of all attributes managed by this authority AA_k. It chooses three random numbers $\alpha_k, \beta_k, \gamma_k \in \mathbb{Z}_p$ as the authority secret key $\mathsf{SK}_k = (\alpha_k, \beta_k, \gamma_k)$. For each attribute $x_k \in S_{A_k}$, the authority generates a public attribute key as $\mathsf{PK}_{x_k} = (g^{v_{x_k}} H(x_k))^{\gamma_k}$ by implicitly choosing an attribute version key as $\mathsf{VK}_{x_k} = v_{x_k}$. The AA_k also computes the authority public key as

   $$\mathsf{PK}_k = \left(e(g, g)^{\alpha_k}, \; g^{\frac{1}{\beta_k}}, \; g^{\frac{\gamma_k}{\beta_k}} \right).$$

   All the public attribute keys are published on the public bulletin board of AA_k, together with the authority public key PK_k.

4.3.2.2 Secret Key Generation by *AAs*

For every user $U_j(j \in S_U)$, each $AA_k(k \in S_A)$ first authenticates whether this user is a legal user by verifying the certificate of the user. It decrypts the item $En_{sk_{CA}}(uid_j, u_j, g^{1/z_j})$ in the certificate $Cert(uid_j)$ by using vk_{CA} and authenticates the user. If the user is not a legal user, it aborts. Otherwise, the AA_k assigns a set of attributes $S_{j,k}$ to this user according to its role or identity in its administration domain. Then, the AA_k runs the secret key generation algorithm SKeyGen to generate the user's secret key $SK_{j,k}$ as

$$\mathsf{SK}_{j,k} = (\, K_{j,k} = g^{\frac{\alpha_k}{z_j}} \cdot g^{au_j} \cdot g^{\frac{a}{\beta_k}t_{j,k}}, \; L_{j,k} = g^{\frac{\beta_k}{z_j}t_{j,k}}, \; R_{j,k} = g^{at_{j,k}},$$

$$\forall x_k \in S_{j,k} : K_{j,x_k} = g^{\frac{\beta_k \gamma_k}{z_j}t_{j,k}} \cdot (g^{v_{x_k}} \cdot H(x_k))^{\gamma_k \beta_k u_j} \,).$$

where $j \in S_U$, $k \in S_A$, and $t_{j,k}$ is a random number in $\mathbb{Z}_p$.

4.3.2.3 Data Encryption by Owners

The owner first encrypts the data component with a content key by using symmetric encryption methods. It then runs the encryption algorithm Encrypt to encrypt the content key. It takes as inputs the system parameter, the public keys, the content key κ and an access structure (M, ρ) over all the selected attributes from the involved *AAs*. Let M be a $l \times n$ matrix, where l denotes the total number of all the attributes. The function ρ associates rows of M to attributes.

The encryption algorithm first chooses a random encryption exponent $s \in \mathbb{Z}_p$ and chooses a random vector $\mathbf{v} = (s, y_2, \ldots, y_n) \in \mathbb{Z}_p^n$, where $y_2, \ldots, y_n$ are used to share the encryption exponent s. For $i = 1$ to l, it computes $\lambda_i = \mathbf{v} \cdot M_i$, where M_i is the vector corresponding to the i-th row of M. Then, it randomly chooses $r_1, r_2, \ldots, r_l \in \mathbb{Z}_p$ and computes the ciphertext as

$$\mathsf{CT} = (\, C = \kappa \cdot (\prod_{k \in I_A} e(g, g)^{\alpha_k})^s, \; C' = g^s, \; C'' = g^{\frac{s}{\beta_k}},$$

$$\forall i = 1 \; tol : C_i = g^{a\lambda_i} \cdot ((g^{v_{\rho(i)}} H(\rho(i)))^{\gamma_k})^{-r_i},$$

$$D_{1,i} = g^{\frac{r_i}{\beta_k}}, \; D_{2,i} = g^{-\frac{\gamma_k}{\beta_k}r_i}, \; \rho(i) \in S_{A_k} \,).$$

4.3.2.4 Data Decryption by Users (with the Help of Cloud Server)

All the legal users in the system can query any interested encrypted data from the cloud server. But only when the user's attributes satisfy the access structure embedded in the ciphertext, he/she can decrypt the content key and use it to further decrypt the data component. The decryption phase consists of two steps:

- **Step 1. Token Generation by Cloud Server**
  The user $U_j (j \in S_U)$ sends its secret keys $\{SK_{j,k}\}_{k \in S_A}$ to the server and asks the server to compute a decryption token for the ciphertext CT by running the token generation algorithm TKGen. Only when the attributes the user U_j possesses satisfy the access structure defined in the ciphertext CT, the server can successfully compute the correct decryption token TK.

  Let $I = \{I_{A_k}\}_{k \in I_A}$ be the whole index set of all the attributes involved in the ciphertext, where $I_{A_k} \subset \{1, \ldots, l\}$ is the index subset of the attributes from the AA_k, defined as $I_{A_k} = \{i : \rho(i) \in S_{A_k}\}$. Let $N_A = |I_A|$ be the number of AAs involved in the ciphertext. It chooses a set of constants $\{w_i \in \mathbb{Z}_p\}_{i \in I}$ and reconstructs the encryption exponent as $s = \sum_{i \in I} w_i \lambda_i$ if $\{\lambda_i\}$ are valid shares of the secret s according to M.

  The algorithm computes the decryption token TK as

  $$
  \begin{aligned}
  TK &= \prod_{k \in I_A} \frac{e(C', K_{j,k}) \cdot e(R_{j,k}, C'')^{-1}}{\prod_{i \in I_{A_k}} \left(e(C_i, GPK_{U_j}) \cdot e(D_{1,i}, K_{j,\rho(i)}) \cdot e(D_{2,i}, L_{j,k}) \right)^{w_i N_A}} \\
  &= \frac{e(g,g)^{au_j s N_A} \cdot \prod_{k \in I_A} e(g,g)^{\frac{\alpha_k}{z_j} s}}{e(g,g)^{u_j a N_A \sum_{i \in I} \lambda_i w_i}} \\
  &= \prod_{k \in I_A} e(g,g)^{\frac{\alpha_k}{z_j} s}.
  \end{aligned}
  $$

  It outputs the decryption token TK for the ciphertext CT and sends it to the user U_j.
- **Step 2. Data Decryption by Users**
  Upon receiving this decryption token TK, the user U_j can use it to decrypt the ciphertext together with its global secret key $GSK_{U_j} = z_j$ as

  $$
  \kappa = \frac{C}{TK^{z_j}}.
  $$

  Then, the user can use the content key κ to further decrypt the encrypted data component.

4.3.3 Efficient Attribute Revocation for DAC-MACS

Suppose an attribute $\tilde{x}_k$ of the user U_μ is revoked from the AA_k. The attribute revocation includes three phases: *Update Key Generation by AAs*, *Secret Key Update by Non-revoked Users*[3] and *Ciphertext Update by Cloud Server*. The secret key update can prevent the revoked user from decrypting the new ciphertexts which are encrypted by the new public attribute keys (Backward Security). The ciphertext update can make sure that the newly joined user can still access the previous data which is published before it joins the system, when its attributes satisfy the access policy associated with the ciphertext (Forward Security).

4.3.3.1 Update Key Generation by *AAs*

The corresponding authority AA_k runs the update key generation algorithm UKeyGen to compute the update keys. The algorithm takes as inputs the authority secret key SK_k, the current attribute version key $v_{\tilde{x}_k}$ and the user's global public keys GPK_{U_j}. It generates a new attribute version key $VK'_{\tilde{x}_k} = v'_{\tilde{x}_k}$. It first calculates the Attribute Update Key as $AUK_{\tilde{x}_k} = \gamma_k(v'_{\tilde{x}_k} - v_{\tilde{x}_k})$, then it applies this $AUK_{\tilde{x}_k}$ to compute the user's Key Update Key

$$KUK_{j,\tilde{x}_k} = g^{u_j \beta_k \cdot AUK_{\tilde{x}_k}}$$

and the Ciphertext Update Key as

$$CUK_{\tilde{x}_k} = \frac{\beta_k}{\gamma_k} \cdot AUK_{\tilde{x}_k}.$$

Then, the AA_k updates the public attribute key of the revoked attribute $\tilde{x}_k$ as

$$PK'_{\tilde{x}_k} = PK_{\tilde{x}_k} \cdot g^{AUK_{\tilde{x}_k}}$$

and broadcasts a message for all the owners that the public attribute key of the revoked attribute $\tilde{x}_k$ is updated. Then, all the owners can get the new public attribute key for the revoked attribute from the public board of AA_k. It outputs both the user's key update key $KUK_{j,\tilde{x}_k}(j \in S_U, j \neq \mu, \tilde{x}_k \in S_{j,k})$ and the ciphertext update key $CUK_{\tilde{x}_k}$.

4.3.3.2 Secret Key Update by Non-Revoked Users

For each non-revoked user $U_j(j \in S_U, j \neq \mu)$ who has the attribute $\tilde{x}_k$, the AA_k sends the corresponding user's key update key $KUK_{j,\tilde{x}_k}$ to it. Upon receiving the user's key update key $KUK_{j,\tilde{x}_k}$, the user U_j runs the key update algorithm SKUpdate to update its secret key as

---

[3] We use *Non-revoked Users* to denote the set of users who possess the revoked attribute but have not been revoked.

$$\mathsf{SK}'_{j,k} = (K'_{j,k} = K_{j,k}, \ L'_{j,k} = L_{j,k}, \ R'_{j,k} = R_{j,k},$$
$$K'_{j,\tilde{x}_k} = K_{j,\tilde{x}_k} \cdot \mathsf{KUK}_{j,\tilde{x}_k}, \ \forall x \in S_u, x \neq \tilde{x} : K'_{j,k} = K_{j,k}).$$

Note that each $\mathsf{KUK}_{j,\tilde{x}_k}$ is associated with the *uid*, so that they are distinguishable for different non-revoked users. Thus, the revoked user U_μ cannot use any other user's update keys to update its secret key.

4.3.3.3 Ciphertext Update by Cloud Server

The AA_k sends a ciphertext update key $\mathsf{CUK}_{\tilde{x}_k}$ to the server. Upon receiving the $\mathsf{CUK}_{\tilde{x}_k}$, the server runs the ciphertext update algorithm CTUpdate to update all the ciphertexts which are associated with the revoked attribute $\tilde{x}_k$. It takes inputs as the current ciphertext CT and the $\mathsf{CUK}_{\tilde{x}_k}$. It only needs to update only a few components of the ciphertext, which are associated with the revoked attribute $\tilde{x}_k$. The new ciphertext CT' is published as

$$\mathsf{CT}' = (C = \kappa \cdot (\prod_{k \in I_A} e(g, g)^{\alpha_k})^s, \ C' = g^s, \ C'' = g^{\frac{s}{\beta_k}},$$
$$\forall i = 1 \ to \ l : \ if \ \rho(i) \neq \tilde{x}_k : \ C_i = g^{a\lambda_i} \cdot ((g^{v_{x_k}} H(x_k))^{\gamma_k})^{-r_i},$$
$$D_{1,i} = g^{\frac{r_i}{\beta_k}}, \ D_{2,i} = g^{-\frac{\gamma_k}{\beta_k}r_i},$$
$$if \ \rho(i) = \tilde{x}_k : \ C'_i = C_i \cdot D_{2,i}^{\mathsf{CUK}_{\tilde{x}_k}},$$
$$D_{1,i} = g^{\frac{r_i}{\beta_k}}, \ D_{2,i} = g^{-\frac{\gamma_k}{\beta_k}r_i}).$$

DAC-MACS requires to update only a few components which are associated with the revoked attribute, while the other components are not changed. This can greatly improve the efficiency of attribute revocation.

The ciphertext update not only can guarantee the backward security of the attribute revocation, but also can reduce the storage overhead on the users (i.e., all the users need to hold only the latest secret key, rather than to keep records on all the previous secret keys).

4.4 Analysis of DAC-MACS

This section provides a comprehensive analysis of DAC-MACS, followed by security and performance analysis.

4.4.1 Comprehensive Analysis

Let $|p|$ be the size of element in the groups with the prime order p. Let t_c be the total number of attributes in a ciphertext and t_u be the total number of attributes of a user. Let n_u denote the number of users in the system. For the revoked attribute x, let $n_{non,x}$ be the number of non-revoked users who hold the revoked attribute and let $n_{c,x}$ be the number of ciphertexts which contain the revoked attribute.

Table 4.1 shows the comparison among DAC-MACS and two existing schemes, which are all based on the ciphertext re-encryption to achieve the attribute revocation. From the table, we can see that DAC-MACS incurs less computation cost for the decryption on the user and less communication cost for the revocation. In DAC-MACS, the attribute revocation is controlled and enforced by each AA independently, but the ciphertexts are updated by the semi-trusted server, which can greatly reduce the workload on the owners. For the security of attribute revocation, DAC-MACS can achieve both forward security and backward security. The cloud server in DAC-MACS is required to be semi-trusted. Even if the cloud server is not semi-trusted in some scenarios, the server will not update the ciphertexts correctly. In this situation, the forward security cannot be guaranteed, but DAC-MACS can still achieve the backward security.

4.4.2 Security Analysis

Under the security model defined in Sect. 4.2.3, we conclude the security analysis into the following theorems:

Theorem 4.1 *When the decisional q-parallel BDHE assumption holds, no polynomial time adversary can selectively break DAC-MACS with a challenge matrix of size $l^* \times n^*$, where $n^* < q$.*

Proof Suppose we have an adversary $\mathcal{A}$ with non-negligible advantage $\varepsilon = Adv_{\mathcal{A}}$ in the selective security game against the construction of DAC-MACS and suppose it chooses a challenge matrix M^* with the dimension at most $q - 1$ columns. In the security game, the adversary can query any secret keys and update keys that cannot be used for decryption in combination with any keys it can obtain from the corrupted AAs. With these constraints, the security game in multi-authority systems can be treated equally to the one in single authority systems. Therefore, we can build a simulator $\mathcal{B}$ that plays the decisional q-parallel BDHE problem with non-negligible advantage as follows.

Init. The simulator takes in the q-parallel BDHE challenge $\mathbf{y}$, T. The adversary gives the algorithm the challenge access structure (M^*, ρ^*), where M^* has n^* columns.

Setup. The simulator runs the CASetup and AASetup algorithm, and gives g to the adversary. The adversary chooses a set of $S'_A \subset S_A$ of corrupted authorities,

Table 4.1 Comprehensive comparison of CP-ABE with attribute revocation schemes

Scheme	Authority	Computation		Revocation message ($|p|$)	Revocation security		Revocation controller	Ciphertext updater
		Encrypt	Decrypt[a]		Backward	Forward		
Hur's [11]	Single	$O(t_c + \log n_u)$	$O(t_u)$	$O(n_{non,x} \log \frac{n_u}{n_{non,x}})$	Yes	Yes	Server[b]	Server[b]
DACC [22]	Multiple	$O(t_c)$	$O(t_u)$	$O(n_{c,x} \cdot n_{non,x})$	Yes	No	Owner	Owner
DAC-MACS	Multiple	$O(t_c)$	$O(1)$	$O(n_{non,x})$	Yes	Yes	AA	Server[c]

[a]The decryption computation on the user; [b]The server is fully trusted; [c]The server is semi-trusted

and reveals these to the simulator. For each uncorrupted authority $AA_k (k \in S_A - S'_A)$, the simulator randomly chooses $\alpha'_k, \beta_k, \gamma_k \in \mathbb{Z}_p (k \in S_A - S'_A)$ and implicitly sets $\alpha_k = \alpha'_k + a^{q+1}$ by letting

$$e(g, g)^{\alpha_k} = e(g^a, g^{a^q})e(g, g)^{\alpha'_k}. \tag{4.1}$$

Then, we describe how the simulator programs the random oracle H by building a table. Consider a call to $H(x)$, if $H(x)$ was already defined in the table, then the oracle returns the same answer as before. Otherwise, begin by choosing a random value d_x. Let X denote the set of indices i, such that $\rho^*(i) = x$. In other words, all the row indices in the set X match the same attribute x. The simulator programs the oracle as

$$H(x) = g^{d_x} \prod_{i \in X} g^{a^2 M^*_{i,1}/b_i} \cdot g^{a^3 M^*_{i,2}/b_i} \cdots g^{a^{n^*+1} M^*_{i,n}/b_i}. \tag{4.2}$$

Note that if $X = \emptyset$ then we have $H(x) = g^{d_x}$. Also note that the response from the oracle are distributed randomly due to the g^{d_x} value.

The simulator also randomly chooses two numbers $\beta_k, \gamma_k \in \mathbb{Z}_p$. Then, it generates the public key of each uncorrupted authority AA_k as

$$PK_k = \left(e(g, g)^{\alpha_k}, g^{\frac{1}{\beta_k}}, g^{\frac{\gamma_k}{\beta_k}} \right).$$

The public attribute keys PK_{x_k} can be simulated by randomly choosing a version number $v_{x_k} \in \mathbb{Z}_p$ as

$$PK_{x_k} = (g^{v_{x_k} + d_{x_k}} \prod_{i \in X} g^{a^2 M^*_{i,1}/b_i} \cdot g^{a^3 M^*_{i,2}/b_i} \cdots g^{a^{n+1} M^*_{i,n}/b_i})^{\gamma_k}.$$

The simulator defined a user identity uid to the adversary. The simulator chooses two random numbers $u'_{uid}, z_{uid} \in \mathbb{Z}_p$. Then, it sets $GSK_{uid} = z_{uid}$ and implicitly sets $u_{uid} = u'_{uid} - \frac{a^q}{z_{uid}}$ by setting

$$GPK_{uid} = g^{u'_{uid}} (g^{a^q})^{-\frac{1}{z_{uid}}}$$

The simulator then sends the global public/secret key pairs (GPK_{uid}, GSK_{uid}) to the adversary.

Phase 1. In this phase, the simulator answers secret key queries and update key queries from the adversary. Suppose the adversary makes secret key queries by submitting pairs (uid, S_k) to the simulator, where S_k is a set of attributes belonging to an uncorrupted authority AA_k. Suppose S_k does not satisfy M^* together with any keys that can obtain from corrupted authorities.

The simulator finds a vector $\mathbf{w} = (w_1, w_2, \ldots, w_{n*}) \in \mathbb{Z}_p^{n*}$, such that $w_1 = -1$ and for all i where $\rho^*(i) \in S_k$ we have that $\mathbf{w} \cdot M_i^* = 0$. By the definition of a LSSS, such a vector must exist, since S_k does not satisfy M^*.

The simulator then implicitly defines t by randomly choosing a number $r \in \mathbb{Z}_p$ as

$$t_{uid,k} = r + w_1 a^{q-1} + w_2 a^{q-2} + \cdots + w_{n*} a^{q-n*}$$

by setting

$$L_{uid,k} = (g^{\frac{\beta_k}{z_{uid}}})^r \prod_{i=1,\ldots,n*} (g^{a^{q-i}})^{w_i \frac{\beta_k}{z_{uid}}}.$$

The simulator then constructs $R_{uid,k}$ as

$$R_{uid,k} = g^{ar} \cdot \prod_{i=1,\ldots,n*} (g^{a^{q+1-i}})^{w_i}.$$

From the definition of $g^{u_{uid}}$, we find that $g^{au_{uid}}$ contains a term of $g^{a^{q+1}/z_{uid}}$, which will cancel out with the unknown term in $g^{\alpha_k/z_{uid}}$ when creating $K_{uid,k}$. The simulator can calculate

$$K_{uid,k} = g^{\frac{\alpha_k'}{z_{uid}}} g^{au_{uid}'} g^{\frac{ar}{\beta_k}} \cdot \prod_{i=1,\ldots,n*} (g^{a^{q+1-i}})^{\frac{w_i}{\beta_k}}.$$

For the calculation of $K_{x_k,uid,k}(\forall x_k \in S_k)$, if x is used in the access structure, the simulator computes K_{x_k,uid,S_k} as follows.

$$K_{uid,x_k} = (L_{uid,k})^{\gamma_k} \cdot (PK_{x_k})^{\beta_k u_{uid}'} \cdot (g^{a^q})^{-\beta_k \gamma_k (v_{x_k} + d_{x_k})/z_{uid}} \cdot$$

$$\prod_{i \in X} \prod_{j=1,\ldots,n*} \left(g^{a^{q+1+j}/b_i}\right)^{-\beta_k \gamma_k M_{i,j}^*}$$

If the attribute $x \in S_{AID}$ is not used in the access structure. That is there is no i such that $\rho^*(i) = x$. For those attributes, we can let

$$K_{uid,x_k} = (L_{uid,k})^{\gamma_k} \cdot (GPK_{uid})^{\beta_k \gamma_k (v_{x_k} + d_{x_k})}.$$

Towards update key queries, suppose the adversary submits pairs of $\{(uid, x_k)\}$. If the attribute x_k has a new version number v_{x_k}', and uid is an non-revoked users, it then sends back the key update key as

$$KUK_{uid,x_k} = g^{u_j \beta_k \gamma_k (v_{x_k}' - v_{x_k})}.$$

Otherwise, it responses "$\perp$".

Challenge. In this phase, the simulator programs the challenge ciphertext. The adversary gives two messages m_0, m_1 to the simulator. The simulator flips a coin b. It creates

$$C = m_b T \cdot \prod_{k \in I_A} e(g^s, g^{\alpha'_{AID_k}})$$

and $C' = g^s$, $C'' = g^{\frac{s}{\beta_k}}$.

The difficult part is to simulate the C_i values since this contains terms that must be canceled out. However, the simulator can choose the secret splitting, such that these can be canceled out. Intuitively, the simulator will choose random $y'_2, \ldots, y'_{n^*}$ and share the secret s using the vector

$$\mathbf{v} = (s, sa + y'_2, sa^2 + y'_3, \ldots, sa^{n^*-1} + y'_{n^*}) \in \mathbb{Z}_p^{n^*}.$$

It also chooses random values $r'_1, \ldots, r'_l$.

For $i = 1, \ldots, n^*$, let R_i be the set of all $k \neq i$ such that $\rho^*(i) = \rho^*(k)$. That is the set of all other row indices that have the same attribute as row i. The challenge ciphertext components can be generated as

$$D_{1,i} = \left(g^{r'_i} g^{sb_i}\right)^{\frac{1}{\beta_k}}, \quad D_{2,i} = \left(g^{r'_i} g^{sb_i}\right)^{\frac{-\gamma_k}{\beta_k}}.$$

From the vector $\mathbf{v}$, we can construct the share of the secret as

$$\lambda_i = s \cdot M^*_{i,1} + \sum_{j=2,\ldots,n^*} (sa^{j-1} + y'_j) M^*_{i,j}$$

Then, we can simulate the C_i as

$$C_i = \left(g^{v_{\rho^*(i)}} \cdot H(\rho^*(i))\right)^{\gamma_k r'_i} \cdot \left(\prod_{j=1,\ldots,n^*} g^{aM_{i,j}y_j}\right) \cdot$$

$$\left(g^{b_i s}\right)^{-\gamma_k(v_{\rho^*(i)} + d_{\rho^*(i)})} \cdot \left(\prod_{k \in R_i} \prod_{j=1,\ldots,n^*} (g^{a^j s(b_i/b_k)})^{\gamma_k M^*_{k,j}}\right).$$

Phase 2. Same as Phase 1.

Guess. The adversary will eventually output a guess b' of b. If $b' = b$, the simulator then outputs 0 to show that $T = e(g, g)^{a^{q+1}s}$; otherwise, it outputs 1 to indicate that it believes T is a random group element in $\mathbb{G}_T$.

When T is a tuple, the simulator $\mathcal{B}$ gives a perfect simulation so we have that $Pr[\mathcal{B}(\mathbf{y}, T = e(g, g)^{a^{q+1}s}) = 0] = \frac{1}{2} + Adv_{\mathcal{A}}$. When T is a random group element the message m_b is completely hidden from the adversary and we have at

$Pr[\mathcal{B}(\mathbf{y}, T = e(g, g)^{a^{q+1}s}) = 0] = \frac{1}{2}$. Therefore, $\mathcal{B}$ can play the decisional q-parallel BDHE game with non-negligible advantage. $\qquad\qquad\square$

Theorem 4.2 *DAC-MACS is secure against the collusion attack.*

Proof In DAC-MACS, each user in the system is assigned with a global unique identity *uid*, and all the secret keys issued to the same user from different *AA*ys are associated with the *uid* of this user. Thus, it is impossible for two or more users to collude and decrypt the ciphertext. Moreover, due to the unique *aid* of each *AA*, all the attributes are distinguishable, even though some *AA*s may issue the same attribute. This can prevent the user from replacing the components of a secret key issued by an *AA* with those components from other secret keys issued by another *AA*. $\qquad\square$

Privacy-Preserving Guarantee Due to the decryption outsourcing, the server can get the users' secret keys. However, the server still cannot decrypt the ciphertext without the knowledge of the users' global secret keys. Moreover, the ciphertext update is done by using the proxy re-encryption method, thus the server does not need to decrypt the ciphertext.

4.4.3 Performance Analysis

We conduct the performance analysis between DAC-MACS and Ruj's DACC under the metrics of *Storage Overhead*, *Communication Cost* and *Computation Cost*.

4.4.3.1 Storage Overhead

The storage overhead is one of the most significant issues of the access control scheme in cloud storage systems. Suppose there are N_A *AA*s in the system. Let $|p|$ be the element size in the $\mathbb{G}$, $\mathbb{G}_T$, $\mathbb{Z}_p$. Let $n_{a,k}$ and $n_{a,k,uid}$ denote the total number of attributes managed by AA_k and the number of attributes assigned to the user with *uid* from AA_k respectively. We compare the storage overhead on each entity in the system, as shown in Table 4.2.

In DAC-MACS, the storage overhead on each AA_k consists of the version number of each attribute and the authority secret key. From Table 4.2, we can see that DAC-MACS incurs less storage overhead on each AA_k than Ruj's DACC, which consists of the secret keys for all the attributes. The public parameters contribute the main storage overhead on the owner. Besides, Ruj's DACC also requires the owner to hold the encryption secret for every ciphertext in the system, because the owner is required to re-encrypt the ciphertexts. This incurs a heavy storage overhead on the owner, especially when the number of ciphertext is large in cloud storage systems. The storage overhead on each user in DAC-MACS comes from the global secret key issued by the CA and the secret keys issued by all the *AA*s. However, in Ruj's DACC, the storage overhead on each user consists of both the secret keys issued by

Table 4.2 Comparison of storage overhead

Entity	Ruj's DACC [22]	DAC-MACS
AA_k	$2n_{a,k}\lvert p\rvert$	$(n_{a,k}+3)\lvert p\rvert$
Owner	$(n_c + 2\sum_{k=1}^{N_A} n_{a,k})\lvert p\rvert$	$(3N_A + 1 + \sum_{k=1}^{N_A} n_{a,k})\lvert p\rvert$
User	$(n_{c,x} + \sum_{k=1}^{N_A} n_{a,k,uid})\lvert p\rvert$	$(3N_A + 1 + \sum_{k=1}^{N_A} n_{a,k,uid})\lvert p\rvert$
Server	$(3t_c + 1)\lvert p\rvert$	$(3t_c + 3)\lvert p\rvert$

n_c total number of ciphertexts on the cloud server
$n_{c,x}$ number of ciphertexts contains x
t_c total number of attributes in the ciphertext

all the AAs and the ciphertext components that associated with the revoked attribute, because when the ciphertext is re-encrypted, some of its components related to the revoked attributes should be sent to each non-revoked user who holds the revoked attributes. The ciphertexts contribute the main storage overhead on the server (here we do not consider the encrypted data which are encrypted by symmetric content keys).

4.4.3.2 Communication Cost

The communication cost of the general access control is almost the same between DAC-MACS and Ruj's DACC. Here, we only compare the communication cost of attribute revocation, as shown in Table 4.3. It is easily to find that the communication cost of attribute revocation in Ruj's scheme is linear to the number of ciphertexts which contain the revoked attributes. Due to the large number of ciphertext in cloud storage system, Ruj's scheme incurs a heavy communication cost for attribute revocation.

4.4.3.3 Computation Cost

The computation time of encryption, decryption and ciphertext re-encryption/update are evaluated by simulating both DAC-MACS and Ruj's DACC. The simulations are conducted on a Linux system with an Intel Core 2 Duo CPU at 3.16 GHz and 4.00 GB RAM. The code uses the Pairing-Based Cryptography library version 0.5.12

Table 4.3 Comparison of communication cost for attribute revocation

Operation	Ruj's DACC [22]	DAC-MACS
Key update	N/A	$n_{non,x}\lvert p\rvert$
Ciphertext update	$(n_{c,x} \cdot n_{non,x} + 1)\lvert p\rvert$	$\lvert p\rvert$

$n_{non,x}$ number of non-revoked users who hold x
$n_{c,x}$ number of ciphertexts which contain x

to simulate the access control schemes. The symmetric elliptic curve α-curve is used in the simulation, where the base field size is 512-bit and the embedding degree is 2. The α-curve has a 160-bit group order, which means p is a 160-bit length prime. All the simulation results are the mean of 20 trials.

We compare the computation efficiency of both encryption and decryption in two criteria: the number of authorities and the number of attributes per authority, as shown in Fig. 4.2. Figure 4.2a describes the comparison of encryption time on the owner versus the number of AAs, where the involved number of attributes from each AA is set to be 10. Figure 4.2b gives the comparison of encryption time on the owner versus the number of attributes from each AA, where the involved number of AAs is set to be 10. Suppose the user has the same number of attributes from each AA. Figure 4.2c shows the comparison of decryption time on the user versus the number of AAs, where the number of attributes the user holds from each AA is set to be 10. Figure 4.2d describes the comparison of decryption time on the user versus the number of attributes the user holds from each AA, where the number of authority for the user is fixed to be 10. Figure 4.2e gives the comparison of ciphertext re-encryption/update versus the number of revoked attributes appeared in the ciphertext.

The simulation results show that DAC-MACS incurs less computation cost on the encryption of owners, the decryption of users and the re-encryption of ciphertexts.

4.5 Related Work

Cryptographic techniques are well applied to access control for remote storage systems [7, 13, 20]. To prevent the untrusted servers from accessing sensitive data, traditional methods [1, 6] usually encrypt the data and only the users who hold valid keys can decrypt and access the data. Then, the data access control becomes the matter of key distribution. These methods require complicated key management schemes and the data owners have to stay online all the time to deliver the keys to new user in the system. Moreover, these methods incur high storage overhead on the server, because the server should store multiple encrypted copies of the same data for users with different keys. Some methods [5, 24] deliver the key management and distribution from the data owners to the remote server under the assumption that the server is trusted. However, the server is not fully trusted in cloud storage systems and thus these methods cannot be applied to data access control for cloud storage systems.

Attribute-based Encryption (ABE) is a promising technique that is designed for access control of encrypted data. After Sahai and Waters introduced the first ABE scheme [23], Goyal et al. [9] formulated the ABE into two complimentary forms: Key-Policy ABE (KP-ABE) and Ciphertext-Policy ABE (CP-ABE). There are a number of works used ABE to realize fine-grained access control for outsourced data [12, 26, 11]. These schemes require a trusted authority to manage all the attributes in the system and issue secret keys to users. Since the authority can decrypt all the encrypted data, it becomes a vulnerable security point and the performance bottleneck

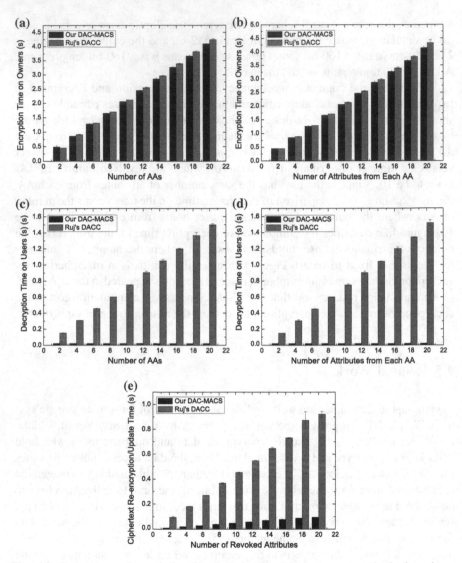

Fig. 4.2 Comparison of encryption, decryption and ciphertext re-encryption/update time. **a** Encryption. **b** Encryption. **c** Decryption. **d** Decryption. **e** Re-encryption/update.

of the system. Moreover, the authority may become the performance bottleneck in the large scale cloud storage systems. In multi-authority cloud storage systems, there are multiple authorities coexist and the users may have attributes from multiple authorities. Existing CP-ABE schemes with single authority are no longer applicable, because no authority is able to verify attributes across different organizations and to issue secret keys to all the users in the system.

Some cryptographic methods are proposed for the multi-authority ABE problem [3, 4, 15, 16, 18, 19], where there are multiple authorities coexist and the users may have attributes from multiple authorities. However, some of them [3, 19] require a global authority, which would be a vulnerable point for security attacks and a performance bottleneck for large scale systems. In [4], the authors remove the central authority by using a distributed PRF (pseudo-random function) but it only support strict "AND" policy of pre-determined authorities. Lin et al. [18] proposed a decentralized scheme based on threshold mechanism. In this scheme, the set of authorities is pre-determined and it requires the interaction among the authorities during the system setup. In [15], Lewko et al. proposed a new comprehensive scheme, which does not require any central authority. It is secure against any collusion attacks and it can process the access policy expressed in any Boolean formula over attributes. However, their method is constructed in composite order bilinear groups that incurs heavy computation cost. They also proposed a multi-authority CP-ABE scheme constructed in prime order group, but they did not consider attribute revocation problem.

There are a number of works about the revocation in ABE systems in the cryptography literature [2, 8, 14, 21, 25]. However, these methods either only support the user level revocation or rely on the server to conduct the attribute revocation. Moreover, these attribute revocation methods are designed only for ABE systems with single authority. Ruj et al. [22] designed a DACC scheme and proposed an attribute revocation method for the Lewko and Waters' decentralized ABE scheme. However, their attribute revocation method incurs a heavy communication cost since it requires the data owner to transmit a new ciphertext component to every non-revoked user. Li et al. [17] proposed an attribute revocation method for multi-authority ABE systems, but their methods is only for KP-ABE systems.

Green et al. [10] proposed two ABE schemes that outsource the decryption to the server. In their schemes, the authority separate the traditional secret key into a user secret key and a transformation key. However, their schemes are designed only for the single authority systems and do not support for the multi-authority systems. That is because each authority may generate different user's secret key, such that the transformation keys cannot be combined together to transform the ciphertext into a correct intermediate value.

4.6 Conclusion

In this chapter, we described an effective data access control scheme for multi-authority cloud storage systems, DAC-MACS. We also described a new multi-authority CP-ABE scheme, in which the main computation of decryption is outsourced to the server. We further presented an efficient attribute revocation method that can achieve both forward security and backward security. The attribute revocation methods incur less communication cost and less computation cost of the revocation, where only those components associated with the revoked attribute in secret keys and ciphertexts need to be updated.

References

1. Benaloh, J., Chase, M., Horvitz, E., Lauter, K.: Patient controlled encryption: ensuring privacy of electronic medical records. In: Proceedings of the first ACM Cloud Computing Security Workshop (CCSW'09), pp. 103–114. ACM (2009)
2. Bethencourt, J., Sahai, A., Waters, B.: Ciphertext-policy attribute-based encryption. In: Proceedings of the 2007 IEEE Symposium on Security and Privacy (S&P'07), pp. 321–334. IEEE Computer Society (2007)
3. Chase, M.: Multi-authority attribute based encryption. In: Proceedings of the 4th Theory of Cryptography Conference on Theory of Cryptography (TCC'07), pp. 515–534. Springer (2007)
4. Chase, M., Chow, S.S.M.: Improving privacy and security in multi-authority attribute-based encryption. In: Proceedings of the 16th ACM Conference on Computer and Communications Security (CCS'09), pp. 121–130. ACM (2009)
5. Damiani, E., di Vimercati, S.D.C., Foresti, S., Jajodia, S., Paraboschi, S., Samarati, P.: Key management for multi-user encrypted databases. In: Proceedings of the 2005 ACM Workshop On Storage Security and Survivability (StorageSS'05), pp. 74–83. ACM (2005)
6. Dong, C., Russello, G., Dulay, N.: Shared and searchable encrypted data for untrusted servers. J. Comput. Secur. **19**(3), 367–397 (2011)
7. Goh, E.J., Shacham, H., Modadugu, N., Boneh, D.: Sirius: Securing remote untrusted storage. In: Proceedings of the Network and Distributed System Security Symposium (NDSS'03). The Internet Society (2003)
8. Goyal, V., Jain, A., Pandey, O., Sahai, A.: Bounded ciphertext policy attribute based encryption. In: Proceedings of the 35th International Colloquium on Automata, Languages and Programming (ICALP'08), pp. 579–591. Springer (2008)
9. Goyal, V., Pandey, O., Sahai, A., Waters, B.: Attribute-based encryption for fine-grained access control of encrypted data. In: Proceedings of the 13th ACM Conference on Computer and Communications Security (CCS'06), pp. 89–98. ACM (2006)
10. Green, M., Hohenberger, S., Waters, B.: Outsourcing the decryption of ABE ciphertexts. In: Proceedings of the 20th USENIX Security Symposium. USENIX Association (2011)
11. Hur, J., Noh, D.K.: Attribute-based access control with efficient revocation in data outsourcing systems. IEEE Trans. Parallel Distrib. Syst. **22**(7), 1214–1221 (2011)
12. Jahid, S., Mittal, P., Borisov, N.: Easier: encryption-based access control in social networks with efficient revocation. In: Proceedings of the 6th ACM Symposium on Information, Computer and Communications Security (ASIACCS'11), pp. 411–415. ACM (2011)
13. Kallahalla, M., Riedel, E., Swaminathan, R., Wang, Q., Fu, K.: Plutus: Scalable secure file sharing on untrusted storage. In: Proceedings of the 2nd USENIX Conference on File and Storage Technologies (FAST'03). USENIX (2003)
14. Lewko, A.B., Okamoto, T., Sahai, A., Takashima, K., Waters, B.: Fully secure functional encryption: Attribute-based encryption and (hierarchical) inner product encryption. In: Proceedings of the 29th Annual International Conference on the Theory and Applications of Cryptographic Techniques: Advances in Cryptology—EUROCRYPT'10, pp. 62–91. Springer (2010)
15. Lewko, A.B., Waters, B.: Decentralizing attribute-based encryption. In: Proceedings of the 30th Annual International Conference on the Theory and Applications of Cryptographic Techniques: Advances in Cryptology—EUROCRYPT'11, pp. 568–588. Springer (2011)
16. Li, J., Huang, Q., Chen, X., Chow, S.S.M., Wong, D.S., Xie, D.: Multi-authority ciphertext-policy attribute-based encryption with accountability. In: Proceedings of the 6th ACM Symposium on Information, Computer and Communications Security (ASIACCS'11), pp. 386–390. ACM (2011)
17. Li, M., Yu, S., Zheng, Y., Ren, K., Lou, W.: Scalable and secure sharing of personal health records in cloud computing using attribute-based encryption. IEEE Trans. Parallel Distrib. Syst. (2012)
18. Lin, H., Cao, Z., Liang, X., Shao, J.: Secure threshold multi authority attribute based encryption without a central authority. Inf. Sci. **180**(13), 2618–2632 (2010)

19. Müller, S., Katzenbeisser, S., Eckert, C.: Distributed attribute-based encryption. In: Proceedings of the 11th International Conference on Information Security and Cryptology, pp. 20–36. Springer (2008)
20. Naor, D., Naor, M., Lotspiech, J.: Revocation and tracing schemes for stateless receivers. Electronic Colloquium on Computational Complexity (ECCC) (2002)
21. Ostrovsky, R., Sahai, A., Waters, B.: Attribute-based encryption with non-monotonic access structures. In: Proceedings of the 14th ACM Conference on Computer and Communications Security (CCS'07), pp. 195–203. ACM (2007)
22. Ruj, S., Nayak, A., Stojmenovic, I.: DACC: Distributed access control in clouds. In: Proceeding of the 10th IEEE International Conference on Trust, Security and Privacy in Computing and Communications (TrustCom'11), pp. 91–98. IEEE (2011)
23. Sahai, A., Waters, B.: Fuzzy identity-based encryption. In: Proceedings of the 24th Annual International Conference on the Theory and Applications of Cryptographic Techniques: Advances in Cryptology—EUROCRYPT'05, pp. 457–473. Springer (2005)
24. Wang, W., Li, Z., Owens, R., Bhargava, B.K.: Secure and efficient access to outsourced data. In: Proceedings of the first ACM Cloud Computing Security Workshop (CCSW'09), pp. 55–66. ACM (2009)
25. Waters, B.: Ciphertext-policy attribute-based encryption: an expressive, efficient, and provably secure realization. In: Proceedings of the 4th International Conference on Practice and Theory in Public Key Cryptography (PKC'11), pp. 53–70. Springer (2011)
26. Yu, S., Wang, C., Ren, K., Lou, W.: Attribute based data sharing with attribute revocation. In: Proceedings of the 5th ACM Symposium on Information, Computer and Communications Security (ASIACCS'10), pp. 261–270. ACM (2010)